PENGUIN BOOKS

Get Sh*t Done!

Niall Harbison is from Cookstown and grew up in Brussels. He spent a number of years working as a private chef before starting his first business, a cookery tutorial website, in 2007 at the age of twenty-seven. Though that business failed, he went on to co-found a social media agency, Simply Zesty, which was acquired by UTV in 2012. He is now co-CEO of global online media platform PR Slides, and also growing the hugely popular website Lovin' Dublin. He lives in Dublin.

Get Sh*t Done!

From spare room to boardroom in 1,000 days

NIALL HARBISON

PENGUIN BOOKS

PENGUIN BOOKS

Published by the Penguin Group
Penguin Books Ltd, 80 Strand, London WC2R ORL, England
Penguin Group (USA) Inc., 375 Hudson Street, New York, New York 10014, USA
Penguin Group (Canada), 90 Eglinton Avenue East, Suite 700, Toronto, Ontario, Canada M4P 2Y3
(a division of Pearson Penguin Canada Inc.)
Penguin Ireland, 25 St Stephen's Green, Dublin 2, Ireland (a division of Penguin Books Ltd)
Penguin Group (Australia), 707 Collins Street, Melbourne, Victoria 3008, Australia
(a division of Pearson Australia Group Pty Ltd)
Penguin Books India Pvt Ltd, 11 Community Centre, Panchsheel Park, New Delhi – 110 017, India
Penguin Group (NZ), 67 Apollo Drive, Rosedale, Auckland 0632, New Zealand
(a division of Pearson New Zealand Ltd)
Penguin Books (South Africa) (Pty) Ltd, Block D, Rosebank Office Park,
181 Jan Smuts Avenue, Parktown North, Gauteng 2193, South Africa

Penguin Books Ltd, Registered Offices: 80 Strand, London WC2R ORL, England

www.penguin.com

First published 2014
Published in Penguin Books 2014
002

Copyright © Niall Harbison, 2014

The moral right of the author has been asserted

Set in 12.5/14.75pt Garamond MT Std
Typeset by Jouve (UK), Milton Keynes
Printed in Great Britain by Clays Ltd, St Ives plc

A CIP catalogue record for this book is available from the British Library

ISBN: 978–0–241–97016–4

www.greenpenguin.co.uk

MIX
Paper from
responsible sources
FSC® C018179

Penguin Books is committed to a sustainable
future for our business, our readers and our planet.
This book is made from Forest Stewardship
Council™ certified paper.

To my best friends and trusted confidants,
Loz, Buster and Snoop,
who are always there when the shit really hits the fan

Contents

Introduction

The private jet had just touched down at Nice airport. Allowing for the chopper ride, the boss would be on board the boat within minutes. Sixty staff rushed around shining up the polished steel. In the kitchen, I squeezed the fresh oranges and sliced up a mango. I knew what the boss wanted because his PA had emailed me an hour earlier from 37,000 feet. As I looked out of the windows of the grand private yacht I could see the glitz and glamour of Monaco and the circus that is the modern Formula 1 paddock. Our boat was too big to fit into the harbour so we were docked just outside. That morning I had taken delivery of €150,000 worth of fresh food for the three-day visit. I took a deep breath as I heard the rotor blades of the helicopter coming into land on the back of the boat.

Then the radio crackled in the kitchen, saying the boss had been invited to George Lucas's apartment to watch the race and would be eating there instead. My three days of hard work to create an exquisite banquet had just gone down the same tube as the food. I picked up the platters of lobster, Kobe beef and truffled pasta and took them into the mess, where the crew got stuck in eating some of the best food money could buy for their eleven o'clock break.

I was working as a private chef to a billionaire and Monaco was my latest stop in a stint of globetrotting and cooking for celebrities all over the world. We'd come down from the Cannes Film Festival the week before and as soon as we were done here I'd be packing up and flying off to join another boat in Miami.

This was the life I led for four years – from helicoptering across the Galapagos to shopping for lobster in the Caribbean through to cooking for F1 drivers in the pits before a race. People with a lot of money like to hire private chefs to cook their favourite dishes rather than eating in a humble restaurant like the rest of us.

Although cooking for billionaires all over the world will be by far the most interesting story to tell over a few beers in the nursing home when I'm older, I've managed to get a lot of shit done for somebody who has just turned thirty-four. I've sailed around Australia in a forty-foot boat, battled storms across the Atlantic in a 400-foot super yacht, spent six months learning how to snowboard in the French Alps, taught myself to surf on the North Shore in Hawaii, been on safari through the wilds of Africa and swum with sharks in the Caribbean. I've also raised investment of over half a million euros each for three different businesses, appeared on *Dragons' Den* in the UK and sold a start-up business to a PLC at the age of thirty-two for a couple of million. I've generally lived the sort of life most people could only dream of. And I've done all this despite being kicked out of school at the age of seventeen after failing the same year four times in a row, suffering from depression and being a binge-drinking alcoholic.

The reasons for writing this book are very simple. I've never been able to sit down and be taught. If I were tested, the experts would probably say I suffer from ADHD or some other modern affliction. Just like billions of other people, I was not successful in my early years: I was decent at sport but never even close to making a career out of it and although I'd consider myself street-smart, I could never study, get good grades or do well in an exam. In short, I was no different from the vast majority of people on this planet. I've always read, though – everything I could get my hands on – and I taught myself from books, newspapers and through online education. I never had the desire to be taught by others but I've always been fascinated with the world and how some people seem to really go after their goals and achieve things.

While travelling over the last decade I've picked up hundreds of business books and self-help manuals and found that 99 per cent of them are beyond useless. They broadly fall into two categories – lofty tomes written by Harvard scholars, where I lose interest on the third page, or books targeted at self-starting business people, where the content is laughably simplistic and of no use to the reader. I wanted to try something different and I've put this book together as an honest manual for both life and business, drawing on my experiences. In it, I explain how you should be taking more risks, how money is a bullshit metric and why fear of failure is the one thing that holds most of us back. I also share how I've struggled with alcoholism and depression and still managed to follow my dreams and achieve my goals. Not everything in this book is going to work for you, but what it contains has helped me get shit done in my life and get it done really quickly.

The cover of the book says 'from spare room to board-room in 1,000 days', and of everything I've achieved, growing a business from a spare-room enterprise to a company with a staff of fifty-five and offices in three cities in a couple of years – well within 1,000 days – is probably the biggest win I've had professionally. Of course, both life and business are unpredictable, and there isn't an exact method for achieving your goals within 1,000 days, so I'm not going to set out a one-size-fits-all formula. Rather I offer here a combination of advice and principles that will help you achieve your own goals in record time, be they in business or for pleasure, and no matter how crazy or far-fetched they might appear.

This is more than a business book. Rather, it's a manifesto – a menu of approaches and techniques to work and life that have helped me to pursue my goals. Have you always wanted to visit America? Learn how to sail? Get back to playing the sports you loved as a kid? Or simply climb a small mountain? Rather than dreaming about those things but never achieving them, this book explains how you can achieve your dreams. Build a company. Travel. Or maybe just have some cool stories to tell the grandchildren. But whatever you do, remember you only get one life, so you might as well grab it and get shit done!

I

Why we shouldn't be afraid to dream big

It was while I was working for another billionaire that I started to think about trying to create my own remarkable life. I'd travelled with him as his personal chef and I was to cook a banquet for him and his friends in his £4 million Mayfair apartment. He gave me £1,000 in cash in the morning and told me they wanted fresh fish. I spent the whole day running around to source the best produce I possibly could and I cooked an amazing four-course feast for six people. As soon as I finished I was invited in for a drink and my boss gave me some of the best advice I have ever received. He said, 'I'm always watching other people driving to work or on their commute and they all look miserable, like they're dreading going to their jobs. There has to be more to life than that, Niall, and I want to make sure I never end up like that.' Though it could sound like arrogance — a rich prick looking down his nose at perfectly happy people — it didn't come across like that. What he was saying was that you have to be unique and follow your heart.

There are loads of different ways to live your life and you don't have to fall into the rat race like so many others do. You don't need to strive to be a billionaire to escape the rat race, either. Why work sixteen-hour days as a young lawyer putting in your apprenticeship when you could be earning the same if not more doing what you really love outside as a landscape gardener or teaching people how to stay fit as a personal trainer? When I decided to ignore all education I was not only looked down upon by others but also concerned that without an education I'd soon be playing catch-up, and that when my friends had houses in suburbs I'd be stuck in a shitty rented apartment with a dead-end job. That's what the world teaches us will happen if we don't jump through the traditional hoops. As it turned out, I was able to earn more than my friends as a chef on a yacht at twenty-three while also getting to see the world and not having to learn stuff in college that I'd have no use for in the future.

There are hundreds of different routes you could take through life and they don't all involve sticking to a rigid educational path or a career ladder that others have chosen for you. Throughout this book I'll try to shift the goalposts so you can end up doing what you really want to do. By the end of the book you'll be the person sitting on a beach in Greece eating fresh-cooked calamari and enjoying the sun rather than the person wedged against the window on a cold morning in January with your socks wet from the rain and going into a meeting with a boss who treats you like shit.

You are perhaps reading this in a warm apartment or house, dressed in comfy clothes. You might even be reading it on a plane on your iPad or with your feet dangling into a swimming pool on holiday. Most Westerners start life with a huge range of opportunities. At twenty-one, most of us have already won the lottery with a healthy body, wonderful family and friends, and infinite potential. Yet we manage to take the incredible hand we have been dealt and turn it into a life of mundane choices and average experiences.

Recall that 70 per cent of people on our planet still don't have the internet. Two billion people live in abject poverty on less than $2 a day and have to walk miles just for water. You and I only have to walk into the kitchen and turn on a tap to get hot or cold water, or open a well-stocked fridge if we want to eat. If simply feeding their children is a goal for many people in the world then surely we should be setting our sights a little higher than buying a box-set of the latest TV must-see and having a quiet weekend in. We complain about our broadband being too slow, our chips being cold or the bills piling up. We lose track of the fact that whoever is up there is smiling down upon us, offering us incredible success and boundless dreams, while we focus on trivial inconveniences and forget about the bigger picture.

In the Western world our lives are more or less mapped out for us from infancy – from toilet training to graduation, the path is fairly well defined. Then suddenly, in our early twenties, we find ourselves with a little freedom. Many of us then head off for a year's travelling now that we actually have the ability to make choices for ourselves.

The sad thing is that, when we return, we are all told we have to jump on the career ladder 'before it is too late' or 'in case others get ahead'. Now I'm not saying that, if you follow this route, there isn't a great deal of fun to be had along the way, or that there aren't some attractive diversions (studying abroad and achieving sporting success being just two), but I also want to suggest to you some entirely alternative routes. You can certainly get lots done within the conventional framework, but the people who excel in it are the ones who have the most money, power and/or brains. It certainly isn't a level playing field.

Sitting somewhere you don't want to be counting seconds is the worst feeling in the world. Wishing our time away is a waste of life, but it's something millions do every day at work. Here is this thing that we are required to do if we want a decent standard of living and which takes up close to 50 per cent of our waking lives. For many it takes a lot more. On average we work about 120,000 minutes per year. We are defined by work. It shapes everything from our social relationships right through to our earning power and what we can do in our spare time. It defines us, yet many of us absolutely loathe it.

The happiest people I encounter are the people who love work, who have found something that is not forty hours a week of paid labour but rather something they like doing. The core principles around getting shit done are about finding things you enjoy and work should be the very first port of call.

When most of us look for a job we use the completely

wrong metrics. How much does it pay? Is it secure? Are there good benefits? Are there career progression opportunities? I can't begin to explain just how wrong those metrics are when it comes to getting the really important and memorable shit done. Those are the metrics that have been determined by managers and people who are above you in the system and who are determined to keep you locked into their way of thinking. To get you sucked into the rat race where getting the next 3 per cent annual pay review is all that matters.

What about flipping those questions over and asking 'How much fun will I have when I'm there?' or 'What skills will I learn there that could benefit me personally three years down the line when I open my own business?'

There are just two types of life that you can choose: the one that others have planned for you or the one that you actually want. That might seem very black and white, and you probably think that you have as many choices as you want, but it doesn't work like that.

Take the majority of twenty-seven-year-old single girls I know. Because of the way our society works a lot of them are fixated on hooking up with a guy and settling down as quickly as they possibly can because 'the biological clock is ticking' or because 'you don't want to get left on the shelf'. So many people choose partners with whom they are clearly making a compromise rather than actually holding out for a relationship that could be incredible and life-changing.

Some of us might dye our hair, get tattoos, play in a band or move abroad but we are mostly all trying to fit into a rigid framework that others have laid out for us. We are scared to step outside the margins, and although it feels like you are just swimming with the tide it actually makes life much harder difficult when it comes to getting stuff done.

It's difficult, for example, to take six months off work to go and learn how to dive when you are a line manager in a large company or have a second child on the way at the age of thirty. As you get older the traps only get worse as your family grows and you acquire some expensive assets like loans for houses and cars that need to be paid off. Before you know it, the only thing you have to look forward to is another staple of the rigid framework: retirement. With any luck – although it is not guaranteed any more with shrinking pension pots and older retirement ages – you might get to enjoy your life in a second home in the sun and have a few glasses of wine.

I hate to play the pessimist, but the car crash, cancer or financial catastrophe that could crush this delicate life path might happen at any moment. The far-off notional future in which you have financial security might never arrive. For that reason, everything in this book is about getting shit done today.

I'm always surprised by the expectations of parents that their children should stay in the education system for as long as possible, because it discourages young people from shooting for the stars and instead forces the majority into a life of mediocrity. An amazing number of the world's remarkable people didn't fit in at school. Look at Mark Zuckerberg, constantly causing trouble in Harvard before eventually quitting and going off to start up Facebook. Same with the Google founders Sergey Brin and Larry Page, who while at Harvard just dropped out and pursued their dreams. According to his autobiography, Steve Jobs seemed to just drop in and out of college, taking the occasional class but more often than not spending the time stoned and discovering new stuff without taking any of the courses. Twitter founder Evan Williams, Oprah Winfrey, Bill Gates, Ralph Lauren, John Lennon, Lady Gaga and Tom Hanks are just a few of those who have not done too badly for themselves but who decided that their time might be better spent elsewhere than in a classroom being told what to do by others. It can also make sense in financial terms to drop out of college as at the time of writing there are thirty billionaires in the world who are college dropouts.

I don't have many regrets in my life but one of them is that I wasted so many years in my teens doing something I wasn't good at. That was the only time I've ever counted down the minutes. I didn't like learning or being sat in one place and as the clock ticked down I'd watch the hands inch forward, willing them to go faster. I know people do this every day while at work, in class or generally doing things they don't like. I don't know what was triggered in my young mind but at seventeen I thought, *I never want to have this feeling again in my entire life.*

School was a torture because not only could I not concentrate but I also had no outlet for my creative instincts. I'd often get suspended or punished for making up my own entertainment. I remember being especially annoyed one night at boarding school when I sneaked out of bed and over to the library. I had a fascination with geography at the time and I used to secretly borrow atlases and theory books. None of it was on the curriculum but I was learning the names of capital cities, seas and mountain ranges and plotting out all sorts of useless data. In short, I was teaching myself and I used to sit up until two in the morning learning about the places that I hoped to visit one day. I got caught sneaking back from the library one night. I started to explain that I was following up my passion for geography, but the teacher could only see that I had broken the rules and gave me a punishment. Well, I absolutely flipped and I remember saying to him, 'Do you understand English?' (it was a Flemish boarding school) and when he said that he did, telling him to go fuck himself.

I didn't wait around for the punishment because I knew I was in trouble and just stormed up the stairs to my room with him shouting after me. Looking back, the guy was just doing his job but I was struggling to fit into the world of traditional education, and slipping behind smarter people, and here I was getting punished for trying to do something that I thought was good. Just like many of you, I didn't fit in; nor did I feel comfortable with the path laid out for me by others. The more I rebelled the more I was pushed back into the system and punished for trying to escape it.

After secondary school I went on to train as a chef. I didn't drop out of cooking school but there isn't a day that goes by when I don't wish that I had done so. It was two years of my life during which I could have achieved much more had I followed my own instincts. It pains me to say it, but I did it for other people. I did it for my mum and dad. To show that I could actually finish something. I did it because friends and family said that I needed the qualification at the end of it to ensure good employment in the future. It turns out that is bullshit and another white lie peddled by people to keep you on the course they have in mind for you.

I remember talking to my first employer, Conrad Gallagher, who had a Michelin star at the time, and asking him about qualifications and the hiring process. He said that he'd never once looked at a qualification and simply asked a chef to cook a fried egg for him (true – it was what he got me to do). One of the simplest tasks in a kitchen. He said that by watching to see if the chef let the pan heat up to the perfect temperature, seasoned the egg, added a little knob of butter and generally treated it with love he would learn far more about that person than any piece of paper could ever tell him.

In college I spent months of my life learning stuff that I never needed. We'd have challenges like making a bowl of soup and some fresh sandwiches for four fake customers and we'd have from nine in the morning until lunchtime

to do it. You'd learn the theory of why eggs rise in a souf-
flé and what molecule structures work in bread. Just like
in school, I struggled with those simple learning tasks and
quickly found myself slipping behind. Once again people
were telling me that I was a failure and I was constantly
being pulled into the head chef's room for a bollocking.

All that changed after a few months. While most of my
college friends went drinking after their classes I got a job
as I needed to pay the rent. On entering a professional
kitchen for the first time I was blown away. It was an absolute madhouse and couldn't be further removed from the
making minestrone in class with a pensioner chef who
hadn't been in a real kitchen for years. Five minutes into
my first shift I was asked to peel a ten-kilo bag of garlic.
That's a lot of garlic. After a couple of minutes arsing
around with it a chef came over and gave me a pretty
sharp reminder that I had to do it in an hour as service
would be starting and he needed me on something else.
He quickly showed me a technique using the back of my
hand and smashing the cloves open. It improved my effi-
ciency by about 500 per cent. He was about 6'5" and tough
as nails and as he headed off he looked me straight in the
eye and said, 'You better have that whole fucking bag
done or there will be trouble, you little shit.' I raced
through the bag as if my life depended on it, honing the
technique as I went. I didn't miss a second's work and
didn't lift my eyes once from that chopping board. To this
day I have not prepped garlic in any other way.

That incident opened my eyes to how much could be

learned under pressure in a professional environment as opposed to messing around in a fake kitchen learning the Latin names for herbs. There is a place for education, but if you take only one thing from this book, please understand that there are many different ways to skin a cat and sometimes good practical work and teaching yourself on the job is as good a way as any. I went on to become the youngest head chef in Ireland at the age of twenty-one and I did so because I spent my every waking hour working in real kitchens with men at least ten years older than me. While I was learning how to butterfly whole legs of lamb or how to shuck oysters on a busy Friday night for a table of twelve, my college classmates were still learning the physics of boiling water. Going to college actually held back my development. And despite later being employed in a dozen countries around the world I was never once asked to show that piece of paper that everybody told me was so important: put me in any kitchen for two hours and I could cook anybody under the table because I'd worked hard and jumped ahead of my colleagues.

So, if you are reading this book and not happy, *please* stand up to the people telling you that you have to take a certain route. If you are unhappy, choose another path. It's a massively difficult thing to do, but if you are to get meaningful stuff done it is absolutely fundamental to chart your own course. I'm sure that Mark Zuckerberg's, Bill Gates's and Oprah Winfrey's parents all nearly had heart attacks when they heard their kids were dropping out of college. I can imagine crisis meetings being held and extreme pressure exerted in an attempt to alter their 'foolish' decisions. They've all got pretty impressive shit done despite not fitting in with the plans that others had for them.

It was 2006 and I was sitting on a super yacht just off the coast of St Barts, a celebrity hot-spot in the Caribbean. We'd just finished a gruelling two-week charter working sixteen-hour days catering to our demanding client's every whim. We worked both Christmas Day and New Year's Eve with barely a second to ourselves. After that, the crew was completely knackered, and after receiving a $3,000 tip each we hit the town. It was the evening after the night before and we'd been planning the evening's partying. Just a couple of hundred yards away the Red Hot Chili Peppers were playing a private gig and Shakira had been spotted along with Enrique Iglesias and Anna Kournikova. The crew still had tons of cash to play with and was ready for the hair of the dog. But someone had to stay behind to mind the boat and I'd volunteered to do it.

Once they'd all gone, I cracked open a beer and fired up my laptop. I started reading about a new site called YouTube and eventually found it in the search engine after trying everything from uTube to YTubz. The design was terrible but after watching a couple of videos of cats falling off roofs and skateboarders my mind began to race with possibilities. Being a chef, I looked for any cooking videos but remarkably I found only a handful and they were all of pretty horrendous quality. YouTube was only a year old at this stage. Just as I was about to cook my dinner I came up with a plan . . . I'd film myself making a video of how to cook the perfect steak and post it. I ran downstairs to get my shitty digital camera (this was long before the iPhone had been invented) and started filming small chunks as I made a step-by-step video on how to cook the perfect steak. It took me about twenty minutes to film it and I then uploaded all the files to my computer. I'd never edited a video in my life so I quickly fired up some Windows movie maker tutorials and sat there for five hours, learning how to edit and putting music to my first-ever video. It was absolutely awful but I hit the upload button and waited the three hours it took to upload it to the site (the Wi-Fi connections were still pretty slow back then!). The other crew came back absolutely hammered and went to their beds as I added my title and tags and sent my first creation live. I thought it was pretty neat but as this was the days before Twitter, Facebook and other social networks I didn't really have anywhere to post it so just stuck it on my blog and emailed a few friends my first creation. I went to bed after a long and painful eight hours, my first online video in the can.

I woke the next morning to find something very strange had happened. I had over 200 emails in my Hotmail account inbox, where I would usually have three or four at the most. It took me a while to work out what was going on but my video had made the front page of an incredibly popular website of the time called Digg. People were sharing it all over the place, commenting on it and posting it on their own blogs. The video already had 60,000 views, which was an enormous figure for the time. (You can still find that video on YouTube today if you type in 'the perfect steak' and my name.) There were emails from producers and food companies and requests from all over the world for more recipes. My head was spinning.

The term social media wasn't even being used back then, but when I sat there looking at all the alerts pouring in I knew that I had seen the future. Little did I know at the time, but staying up for eight hours that night and creating that video would be the catalyst for two businesses. iFoods would come six months later and we would raise €500,000 for a social network that would be the 'Facebook for foodies' featuring instructional cooking videos.

I'd been awakened to the power of social media and immediately saw the potential for brands to market themselves in this manner, but it would take another three years before I would start Simply Zesty, a social media agency for brands that focused heavily on video and which I would end up selling to UTV in 2012.

I was in the right place at the right time and I got very lucky with that video, but it taught me a very valuable lesson that is at the very core of getting shit done and leading a remarkable life, and that is that you have to take chances, put yourself out there and not have fear. The easy thing to do that night with the whole boat to myself and a stinking hangover would have been to crack open an expensive bottle of wine and fire up a movie on the giant screen and pretend to myself that I was a millionaire and enjoy the luxuries of the yacht. I could have sat up on the top deck in the Jacuzzi drinking champagne without a care in the world and money in my pocket, enjoying the dream life in my mid-twenties, but I decided to try something completely different.

Too often we take the easy route, but by pushing ourselves and never resting on our laurels the biggest opportunities will always present themselves out of nowhere. When people pat me on the back and say that I have achieved so much and am an overnight success I refer them to that video from eight years ago. Nothing happens quickly; my 'overnight success' is actually the result of eight years of remarkably hard work and sacrifices and missed nights out.

The only thing that ever annoys me about my friends is that they say I am lucky. I'm known among them as 'the lucky one'. It annoys me because it couldn't be further from the truth. Many of us rely on luck (the lottery), hope (horoscopes) or history (family connections) to make our dreams come true. You hear people say things like 'You need to be in the right place at the right time' or 'Sure, it was meant to be'. I couldn't disagree more with such statements when it comes to getting shit done; if anything, thinking like that will ensure that life passes you by. We've all been in the pub with a group of friends kicking around business ideas and imagining untold riches if we tried out a certain idea. The simple fact is that the vast majority of us don't realize our dreams or get shit done because we don't do any follow through. Most of us are happy to sit in and watch *The X Factor* on a Saturday night or go for a few pints and watch Monday-night football, yet we are surprised when our businesses don't grow exponentially or our music careers don't take off. If you want to get shit done you need to understand that luck has nothing to do with it. Absolutely nothing. You get out of life only what you put into it.

When I was looking for my first job on a yacht some friends and I stayed for three weeks in a campsite in the south of France, living off baguettes and flasks of red wine at €5 a pop. I had €1,200 to my name and every day from six in the morning we walked up and down the docks, admiring the huge super yachts and looking for a day's work. I got knockback after knockback and after two weeks I was ready to quit. Two of the lads I was with did actually quit and went off to surf in Portugal. I ploughed away and was eventually offered a week's work on pretty much the shittiest boat in the port. We'd hardly ever even leave the quay, the sailing confined to short day trips during which I saw nothing beyond the galley walls. The interfering owners I cooked for came down every night with a white glove and made me polish the stainless steel in the kitchen until it was spotless. They made me feel two feet tall and often joked about the Irish not knowing how to cook. I swallowed my pride even after they sent back plate after plate of perfectly good food and worked me to the bone. On several occasions I nearly walked. I remember one day in particular when I was especially seasick and the owner spotted that and brought me inside from the deck to stand in the vast walk-in fridge. As I stood there watching all the trays and making sure nothing fell off the shelves the boat rocked violently and I resolved that this bastard wouldn't beat me and that I was the bigger man. I kept getting up earlier, working later and generally doing whatever I could to stay in the game. I knew my break would come.

After two weeks of hell and about to give up, I took a call from an agency. Would I like to work freelance on a boat at the Monaco Grand Prix for three days? I jumped at the chance and made my polite excuses and left with a few hundred euros in my pocket. That very same evening I was aboard a new boat with a proper set-up, a great crew and a lovely English captain. I busted my balls and cooked some of the best food I ever had in my life for the lunch banquet. With the guests all gone to watch the race I cleaned the kitchen. The captain popped in and said that their last chef had left suddenly and the owner had been seriously impressed with my food and that he would love to offer me a job. I nearly kissed him when he told me that the money wouldn't be great but that I could make it up in tips. It turned out the money was more than triple what I had been working for with the other prick. I had a job and we were to set sail the next day to Barcelona. My first real job on a yacht and an entry into a whole new world of cooking on the high seas that I had dreamed of as a kid.

Though I'd seen Formula 1 before, nothing could

prepare me for the razzle dazzle of Monaco. I was an F1 fanatic and could hear the cars from my kitchen but I wasn't expecting to see any of the action. As I went out to have a cigarette, though, qualifying for the race was in full swing. I sneaked through a barrier down by the boats and found myself behind some tyres, the only spot on the circuit where nobody else happened to be. As I started to take it all in, around the corner came the red blaze of the mighty Ferrari belonging to Michael Schumacher. He slowed and suddenly veered, crashing into the barrier not even ten yards from me. It wasn't a high-speed crash and Schumacher jumped out of the car and pulled his helmet off. He waved up to the crowd on the hill and walked towards me to skip through a gap and get back to the safety of the pits. I'm still not sure to this day if I dreamed it, or if I've embellished the story in my own mind, but as he walked past he had a rueful smile and gave me a little wink as the only person in the vicinity. As he was quickly surrounded by a media scrum looking for an interview I pinched myself and headed back to the boat on cloud nine.

People always say I'm so lucky and that I get the coolest shit happening to me but I know there isn't one ounce of luck about it. If I hadn't polished that shitty kitchen, bitten my tongue and spent the thirty minutes in that fridge trying not to throw up I would never have been beside that track in Monaco. Getting shit done isn't easy, but you can rule one thing out of the equation and that is luck.

*

Apart from working hard and creating your own luck, helping others is the third principle I try to stick by that keeps reaping dividends. And it can happen in the most unlikely way.

Although I didn't grow up in Dublin, *The Commitments* has always had a special place in my heart. I was particularly captivated by the scene in the bath where the young wannabe band manager, Jimmy Rabbitte, pretended he was getting interviewed on *The Late Late Show* about being the manager of the successful band. I identified with Jimmy and often lay in bed at night dreaming that one day I'd be on the show answering questions about my business prowess. Turning up on Ireland's biggest chat show would mean I had arrived – hardly the most important measure of success, but a personal goal all the same. I suppose you could say that after getting kicked out of school at seventeen and being told by everybody I was stupid, it would be my way of saying, 'Hey look at me. I'm actually quite smart.'

One morning I was incredibly hungover after a night on the tiles and had been asked by Enterprise Ireland to talk to some start-up companies. I was incredibly busy with running my business and keeping fifty staff productive and happy but made a trip down to talk to a roomful of people who had just scraped together enough money to start a business. I cursed my luck the whole way down there and wished I could be back in the comfort of my office messing around online. I'd just sold a business – Simply Zesty – and they wanted me to tell my story.

I didn't have anything prepared and was just going to rattle through some boring slides that I'd used a hundred times before. But as I looked at all the hopeful faces in the crowd I decided that, rather than talk about success, I'd focus on failure and the fact that many in the room would also fail in their bids to create meaningful companies. I explained how I had often failed, what I'd done wrong and how I'd picked myself up again. It wasn't something that I wanted to be doing and it hurt to tell that story but I knew people would get something out of it. It almost felt like therapy, and after the event twelve people queued up to ask me questions. Again I thought to myself, *What the fuck am I doing here?* and started to edge towards the door. I just wanted to crawl into a corner and die. The last person approached and as she started talking all I was thinking was how soon I might get back to my office, or better still to my bed. Then she introduced herself. She was a researcher from *The Late Late Show*. She had loved my story and would I like to go on the show and talk about business and tell them about failure and success? I was floored.

A couple of months later I was in the TV studios with Lauren, my business partner in Simply Zesty. We were like two little schoolchildren as we stood backstage and heard the band kicking off and *Late Late* presenter Ryan Tubridy introducing us as people who had sold a business. As it happened, I had appeared on *The Late Late Show* before, with five other entrepreneurs, but this was different from simply plugging iFoods. I was sitting in the hot seat being asked questions about how we'd made it. When the questions flipped over to Lauren I watched her with immense pride and then took a minute to look out at the people in the audience. I just had a moment to myself where I thought, *Holy shit, this sort of stuff isn't meant to happen to people like me.*

When I drove down to that Enterprise Ireland meeting with all those start-ups to tell them my story I did so selflessly with the hope that maybe I could help one of them someday. But it made a dream come true for me. Doing things that help other people and that are demanding on your own time will often come back and help you a hundred times more in the future. But not always – I've done lots of things that I'll never see a return on – but sitting on that couch was something I'd dreamed of since I was a teenager and one of the few times in my life that I felt I'd achieved something. It might only have been my granny and a few friends who watched it and cared but for me that was getting shit done movie style!

I think about dying a lot. I think about dying every night and I ask myself the same question before I roll over and drift away: *If today was my last day on earth, would I be happy with what I have achieved so far?* The reason I ask myself that question is to constantly push myself and because I know that, if they were honest, 99.99 per cent of people would answer no. I don't always say yes, but I am running at a 70 per cent rate at the moment and always finding ways to get that percentage higher.

When I was twenty-six I saw my grandfather dying. He had cancer and the doctors had told him to pack up his things, leave the hospital and go and get his affairs in order, which is medical speak for *The jig is up; there is nothing more we can do for you.* From start to finish he died in about a couple of weeks. I knew he was going to die, he knew he was going to die, and as I sat with him in his room, the spectre of death hanging over us, the conversations weren't especially light-hearted. It was hard to find the right words and I couldn't help thinking, *This is going to be me one day. Hopefully like him I'll lead a good life, have a wonderful family around me in my last hours and, like him, see it through to at least seventy-eight but my lungs are weak and I'll eventually die too. I'll be the one reliving every moment of my life in slow motion in the depth of night. Why didn't I have more sex? Why didn't I try acid at least once? Why didn't I go back and fight for the girl I really loved? Why didn't I jump out of a plane or take the cruise to Alaska?* Mostly I looked at my granda and I thought, *There are some things that he is definitely not thinking about right now. He isn't thinking why did I not get my 2 per cent pay rise when I deserved it? Why did I let that fucker get away with cutting me off at the lights?*

The biggest fault that many of us have is that we count down the minutes of our lives. We might be in work, in a lecture hall or just at a social event that we have been persuaded to attend by a partner. Look around and you will see it all the time: people looking forward to their holidays; praying for the last few hours to whizz past before the weekend. Why, if we are on this planet for a limited

amount of time, do we spend our time wishing the seconds away?

There is nothing like the clarity of death and realizing
that we are all mortal to focus the mind. Given the choice
in later years to make every decision again, big or small, I
have no doubt that most of us would go for the more
risky and bold choices rather than erring on the side of
caution.

I've always tried to go for the riskier option. That's why
I've ended up sailing up the Australian coast for 500 miles
on a yacht just thirty-eight feet long and nearly dying in
vicious storms. Why I've snowboarded down sides of
mountains off the beaten track in six foot of fresh powder
while guys beside me started little mini avalanches while
we all feared for our lives. Why I've lain flat on my back in
the middle of the Atlantic Ocean, drinking champagne
while holding a girl's hand and looking up at the most
amazing stars in the world, thousands of miles from the
nearest land.

Every time a choice presents itself to me that involves
risk I've taken it and I would urge you to do the same if
you want to get the shit that matters done. It doesn't have
to be the big choices either. It just means going and jumping in the sea at the local beach even though it is only
March. So what if it is cold? You'll always remember that
and you'll never remember flicking through the *Daily Mail*
on your iPad looking at pictures of celebrities in Barbados. Don't go to the same sandwich place you go to every
day and get the BLT but walk fifty yards further and try

that weird little Arab place where all the interesting-looking people queue up. Your day consists of 10,000 tiny choices and each of those choices represents a chance for you either to cop out and take the easy option or to try something new. Watch *The X Factor* or cook a new recipe for friends? Click into Twitter or pick up the phone and make a sales call that could bring success to your business?

Nobody is ever going to take all the risks that present themselves, and we all make mistakes along the way, but you know yourself that you settle for the ordinary so many times on a daily basis. Most people don't like to think about the fact that we are here for a finite amount of time, but acknowledging that and starting to take bigger risks is a key step towards having a remarkable life.

2

To be a success, fail as fast as you can

Steve Jobs failed so badly that he was asked to leave his own company. This was a man who had taken the computer world by storm and who at thirty should have been in the prime of his career. His vision had redefined an entire industry, but because he couldn't make money he ultimately failed. His board voted him out of his executive roles in the company he had built up from a small garage into a global powerhouse and publicly humiliated him in the process. This is the same man who, when he passed away twenty-six years later, was practically canonized for the success he had achieved, the failure long forgotten.

We've all seen the world's biggest bands, such as U2 or Coldplay, performing to 100,000 adoring stadium fans singing along to every lyric of every song, but we didn't see them saving up for that first guitar at fourteen or hauling an amp around dirty clubs and playing to fifteen people at the start of their careers. We didn't see the lads standing in the dole queue or the endless rejections from record companies. We didn't see the goofy-looking teens, derided and belittled while they practised in their parents' garage. We didn't see the band driving across half the country for a gig where nobody showed up. And we didn't see the early band members walking out because success didn't come quickly enough. Because of our reality-TV world that creates instant celebrity we think that success, when it comes, comes overnight.

Michael Jordan, who is without doubt the best basketball player ever, if not the greatest sportsman of his generation, summed it up best when he said: 'I've missed more than 9,000 shots in my career. I've lost almost 300 games. Twenty-six times I've been trusted to take the game-winning shot and missed. I've failed over and over and over again in my life. And that is why I succeed.'

Trace any famous or successful person's career back from its high point, and you'll likely find it littered with failures. Steve Jobs didn't just lie down after his public humiliation but used it as the burning cause of his life to drive him on and make sure it never happened again. There are countless examples of hugely successful people failing and coming back to even bigger success, and it could be argued that the defining moments of Jobs's later career – the launch of the iPhone and the iPad – wouldn't have been achieved without tasting that failure in the first place. It is no coincidence that in his second coming as a CEO not only did he build the best products but he also built the most profitable and valuable company in the world, measured by market capitalization. He had absorbed the failure, hit rock bottom, learned from it and come back a better, more successful person, getting more shit done than ever before.

If you want to be a success, you're going to have to get comfortable with failing. I mean *really* comfortable. Achieving your dreams means failing over and over again – and while none of us lies there at night thinking about how our business or personal goals will come crashing down, that's exactly what we should be doing.

Success is rare, whereas failure is everywhere. If everyone achieved everything they wanted, without failure, the world would be full of gold medallists, rock stars and Oscar winners. You probably won't immediately achieve whatever you were hoping to achieve when you picked up this book. You might not ever achieve it. That's not a perverse thing to say but merely a statistical fact. Because humans don't like talking about failure we banish it from our thoughts – but rather than sugar-coat things, I want to explain why embracing it is crucial to your ultimate success.

We are all so self-aware these days that even after a little accidental trip on the street we refuse all help, stare at the spot that tripped us and hurry away before anybody has the chance to see we have failed at the simple task of walking. When it comes to business, the main reason people don't start one is because they are scared shitless of failure. It's the reason we work in jobs we hate, wasting our lives away. How many times have we sat in a pub tossing around a brilliant business proposition? The next morning it's easier to just laugh it off as a mad idea fuelled by too many pints and we get on with our ordinary lives. Sure, we'd only fail anyway, we tell ourselves.

And no, it isn't easy. But brilliant entrepreneurs and high-achievers do it over and over again. Fail, that is. Bouncing back from failure is like getting a massive kick in the balls and getting straight back up and asking to be kicked again. It's endlessly banging the door down and refusing to take no for an answer. And it's about finding the strength to go on that you didn't think you had. It's shanking a hundred drives on the range before you hit one perfectly. It's watching in dejection as ten soufflés in a row collapse only to see the eleventh rise majestically above the edge of the ramekin. As toddlers trying to walk for the first time, we smash our faces a hundred times before we take those first five magical steps in a row. In fact, the ability to bounce back from constant failure to ultimately succeed can best be demonstrated by a child learning to swim or ride a bike. The older we get, the more aware we all become of failure and what others will think about us and the fewer risks we take.

Every day I see people who are moderately talented but who are achieving great things. The feature that distinguishes them is their willingness to keep taking their knocks. Be it a sports star putting their body on the line over and over again or business people who have tried every conceivable strategy and failed but who keep coming back for more. The hardest part is admitting to yourself that you want to achieve something, and accepting that the route there will be littered by mini failures. It is your inner resolve and determination to keep getting back up after those failures that will see you past the finish post. Failure isn't a conclusion but merely a small stepping stone towards bigger success and getting more shit done.

My first business, iFoods, was the biggest turning point in my life. That was the one I hit upon after filming myself cooking steak on the boat; the instructional website that was supposed to be 'Facebook for Foodies'. I was twenty-six and quit my €8,000-a-month tax-free job cooking for billionaires and threw in €50,000 of my savings. After I sold him the dream my best friend Sean quit his job and put money in as well. Our enthusiasm helped us to raise a total of €150,000 from friends and family, including my dad and my cousin. We were young and keen and we thought we were absolutely bulletproof. Six months later, in 2007, we were up and running. I like to think we were ahead of our time.

We saw spectacular growth at the start and appeared on *Dragons' Den* in the UK. We didn't manage to persuade the Dragons to invest, but the media coverage was just wall-to-wall. With a million people visiting the site after just six months we thought we'd made it big, and raised a further €400,000 from investors. The media, friends and pundits were blowing smoke up our asses and we thought we were great lads with all that money in the bank and certain riches to come. But although we had plenty of users and even more hype, we had one catastrophic hole in our plan: there was no revenue model. We didn't charge for use of the site, meaning we were entirely reliant on advertising – and when that didn't work for us, we were screwed. We pissed through the money with a bunch of ludicrous business decisions and the rot set in. We pivoted more times than a Russian ballerina in search of a business model.

In the end, the money ran out and the fallout ruined my life for about a year. Sean and I stopped speaking, as even though we'd been best friends and inseparable since the age of two, we blamed one another for the failure. There was even talk of legal action.

Losing my own money that I'd worked for was tough, but nowhere near as bad as losing that of my friends and family. They'd bought into my dream and I'd let them down. I felt about as low as I possibly could and switched my phone off, hit the bottle hard and tried to forget it all while convincing myself that my schoolteachers must have been right: I was actually stupid. The buck really does stop with the person who had the idea and who sold the dream — and although my family wouldn't say I'd let them down, I knew I'd really screwed up. It felt rotten.

It was only about six months later that, in hindsight, I started to see all the things I've written about so far. Failing in a business is a bit like doing an MBA: yes, it's an expensive way to learn lessons — but the lessons can be immense. So immense that several venture capitalists, especially in the USA, won't invest in a business unless a founder has already failed. Imagine that: failure is actually a prerequisite to being investable! For many entrepreneurs, failure is like a badge of honour.

It's easier to see the value of failure in retrospect. At the time, it's agonizing. What I dreaded most was walking into a bar and seeing my old mates, the same guys who, after reading the press, presumed we were on track to be billionaires. Surely the ones who slapped us on the back and told us we were deadly would be laughing at us now. I built it up into something monstrous in my head, a whole bunch of fantasies that involved people laughing behind my back at my failure. Now that we'd crashed and burned, people were bound to say 'I told you so' and 'Who did that fucker think he was anyway?'

It was a couple of months before I felt ready to go out and socialize again, but once I did, I was so surprised at the reaction. Nobody was laughing, nobody was lording it over me; in fact, nobody really cared, apart from my really good mates. People are so busy leading their own lives that they don't have time to be worrying about your failures – they have enough of their own to be concerned about. It was then that the weight was lifted from my shoulders. I could breathe again. The world wasn't going to end and I still had food to eat and a bed to sleep in.

But that wasn't all I learned. In fact, it wasn't until many months later, when I was asked to give a talk to some entrepreneurs, that the moral of the story truly sank in. I'd often be asked to speak because I'd both succeeded and failed in business. I had both succeeded in building iFoods and failed to keep it alive. I also didn't mind talking about my experiences. But I was apprehensive when I was told the title was to be 'What I Learned About Failing', and I seriously thought about turning the engagement down. I mean, who wants to stand in front of a roomful of people telling them what a big failure you've been and how you've squandered the last three years of your life and blown a bunch of your family's hard-earned money. But for whatever reason, I decided to go for it. Abandoning my prepared slide show and script, I spilled my guts on failing to a room of sixteen hot start-ups who had raised a lot of cash.

I hadn't intended to be so honest, but the experience did me a world of good. We'd made every mistake in the book. We'd lost a shed load of cash and I'd given up a dream job to start something that had crashed and burned. As the words came out of my mouth and I watched the faces around the room identify with my story of failure, something clicked inside me. There wasn't anything scary about failure in the least. It was normal.

I've never looked back from that moment. As I walked out of that conference room I became a very dangerous man because I realized that failure wasn't as bad as I'd made it out to be in my own head. Fear of failure had stopped me from doing so many things in my life but I knew it was no longer the ordeal I'd imagined it to be. Now that I had experienced it once, I knew I could deal with it. I've failed many times since, but I've failed much faster and always learned a lesson along the way.

It is strange that we are all so crippled by fear, and we're especially fearful of how others will react to our failure. Imagine a friend going for a promotion, a partner setting up a business or a sibling trying to get a place on a really tough college course. Even though they are all setting themselves up for failure, you only want the best for them. We are all there for people we love when they fail. Yet when it comes to us taking a risk ourselves we are petrified of what others will think about us when we fail. We shouldn't be. The only people who want you to fail are your competitors, enemies or people who don't matter to you anyway.

With that in mind, one effective tactic in getting shit done is to use past failures to drive you on to even bigger success. Sports managers have been known to print out comments by opposition coaches or the media and hang them on the walls of their team's dressing room before a game. When iFoods failed there were a tiny minority of people who made derogatory comments and were intent on putting the final nail in the coffin. You have to expect that when you get lots of media attention and when you set yourself up by making big statements about future plans that ultimately end up being completely wrong. If you say things like you are going to be the 'Facebook for foodies' and then end up burning through all your cash and having to slink back into your corner you have to expect some brickbats. The day I finally admitted to myself and the world that the site would be shutting down a handful of people responded with 'I told you so' or 'Good riddance'. I can tell you that, sitting there with my head metaphorically in my hands, those comments really hurt.

I took a screen grab of every one of those comments and saved them to my laptop in a folder I labelled 'Haters'. I didn't know what I was going to do with them, but as my next business, Simply Zesty, grew I looked at them often as I worked late into the night. The haters drove me on.

So, nothing is surer than the fact that you are going to fail and that it is going to be painful. You need to make sure you take a nugget from every failure to spur you on. Write something down. Take a photo. Record a little audio file or video that you keep for yourself to explain how you felt at that very moment. Nothing drives people on more than the thought of failing again and there is absolutely no harm in finding ways to remind yourself of just how bad it felt at the time.

You often hear entrepreneurs who have had spectacular success tell stories of how they were moments from failure, and the emotional roller coaster they've ridden. I had my own experience of that in Simply Zesty, which we later sold to UTV. Just four months before selling we were desperately short of cash. We'd grown fast and hired twenty-five staff but the money wasn't coming in quickly enough to pay the wages. I remember sitting with Ken, our CEO, and looking at the bank balance a day before the wages were due to be paid. We had €400. Yes we were owed over €100,000 by multiple large reputable clients but that was a couple of weeks away and the €400 we had to our name wasn't going to go very far towards paying the staff's mortgages or heating bills or buying their weekly shopping. There are lots of rules in business that you try to stick to but the most fundamental of them is to pay your staff on time. Well, here we were a day away from not only breaking it but doing so in spectacular fashion.

We sat in the boardroom and tried to come up with solutions. Maybe we could delay our VAT payment or ask some of our larger clients for a line of credit. We were already forgoing our own wages and had pushed suppliers to the very edge in terms of paying them. We weren't a bad business or bad business people but we faced the same problem that blights so many small firms and that is poor cash flow. The banks wouldn't talk to us because it was the height of the recession in Ireland and credit was on ice. We banged our heads together for two hours but still didn't have any solutions. In the end we decided to leave it for twenty-four hours and come back and see what could be done the next day. Neither of us was very hopeful.

As I walked out of that boardroom my head was spinning, with failure rearing its ugly head again after the iFoods fiasco. I told myself that maybe I just wasn't meant to be in business after all and that the teachers had been right all along. Not only was I going to let myself down again but here I was with friends and staff working for me who were about to get shafted for their wages. As I walked back to my desk one of the account managers, Trevor, asked if I could sign off on €400 for a client video shoot. I don't know where I found the strength but I looked him straight in the eye and said 'Of course I can, man' and signed the paper.

I didn't sleep that night and came in the next morning hoping that something would finally go our way. And it did: with two days to spare a client lodged a large payment early and we made the wage bill. Indeed, it was a turning point for the whole business as the cash started rolling in and we were secure again.

In business crises like that – flooding, cash-flow issues, a product recall, legal threats – are never far away and you will always be judged by how you manage them. It's easy to drink champagne and high five each other when the times are good but I learned a lot about Ken and myself that week when we were standing naked with our balls against the wall and we held our nerve.

One way to get over failure is to set yourself up for it and share your goals and ambitions publicly. Sharing something with your friends or family and telling them what you want to achieve is often the hardest first step. Even writing down what you want to achieve and admitting to yourself that it is a dream is a seriously big step. Telling yourself or others that you want to be a professional singer, leave your job to be a chef or run a marathon is a big step. Our dreams flash in and out of our heads all the time, but the easiest thing to do is to dismiss them and keep on daydreaming or thinking 'I'll do it one day'. My own technique, and one I would encourage you to use if you want to get shit done, is to share the outrageous or outlandish dreams in as public a way as you possibly can.

Despite dropping out of school and never having

written anything of worth in my life, it had always been a dream of mine to write a book. I'd often get immersed in business books or novels and think to myself I could maybe have a good stab at doing something similar. I kicked the idea around for a few months but it wasn't really going anywhere. One day I woke up and thought, *Fuck it, I'll do this.* I tested the water with a few friends, throwing the idea out there, and most laughed or said I was mad. With something this big, though, I needed more exposure. It would be too easy to brush friends and family off with 'Oh, I'm still working on it'.

So I chose the most public platform of all – social media – and, without having anything more than a seed of an idea in my head, wrote: 'I am publishing a book, it will be in shops in nine months and it will be a bestseller.' I tweeted that sentence to 12,000 people, put it on my Facebook page where my best friends could see it and shared it with anybody who would listen. Those posts are still online today, and the simple little action forced me to write this entire book and achieve a lifetime's ambition. I got a fantastic reaction with lots of encouragement, as you would expect, but when I woke up the next morning I thought to myself, *Fuck! What have I gone and done? How am I going to write a book?*

Sharing something so publicly focused my mind. It gave me no option but to start working on it. The chances were still very high that I would fail at what I was trying to do, but now that I'd made it real I'd have to at least give it a lash. So that very day I started sketching out ideas, thinking of titles and reading up on the world of publishing and how it all worked. I'd have never taken those steps if I hadn't told people I was going to. Without telling people, I'd have gone out to get some food and found something else to keep myself 'busy' with. Turning the crazy thoughts in your head into reality starts by admitting you want to achieve them. By telling people. By having the balls to admit it to yourself. I don't know what your own dream is, but I know you have one. I'm sure my granda had one when he was on that bed taking deep breaths, but he probably had to tell himself that it wasn't going to happen now. I'm not saying that admitting your dream to yourself and others will make it come true, but at least you'll be forced to give it a go.

One thing that you will have to learn is how to fail as fast as you possibly can. Many of us remain in adverse situations far longer than we should just because we are afraid to admit to others that we have failed. I've done so myself. People stay in bad marriages or relationships for the same reason. In all the big failures I've had in my life, the only regret I have is that in nearly all of them I kept failing for longer than I should have. In iFoods we ended up raising over €600,000, and even though we spent it all and the business was about to come crashing down, I wouldn't admit it. When we got to our last €10,000 I should have given up, but instead I put everything on hold, locked myself in my apartment and started working out ways to resurrect the empire and build it back up to what it was and turn it into a success with that last €10,000. Even though I'd have to do everything on my own, and the odds were a thousand to one, I still believed I was going to be the hero at the end of the day and make it a success. Despite every indication to the contrary, from website traffic to bills pouring in right through to the advice from my friends and business people to shut it down, I hung on to that business for at least six months longer than I should have. Of course, all I was doing was postponing the day of execution and the humiliation of having to admit it was over. Had I acknowledged the writing on the wall I could not only have saved myself those months of anguish but also have started to rebuild and put my energy into something much more positive. To get new shit done.

I'm not saying you should give up on things the second the tide starts to turn against you, because the brightest moments in both business and life in general often come straight after the darkest storms, but knowing when to pull the plug and admit failure is absolutely key. I'd love to say there is an infallible formula to distinguish the fine margins between failure and success, but it can only usually be figured out by going with your gut. Failing faster applies to everything you do in your life. We've all been in relationships that are going nowhere but we still try to recapture the 'amazing days we had at the start'. Being ruthless and learning how to fail faster will not only save you further heartache but also free up time to focus on new endeavours and more positive pursuits.

*

The simple way to conquer things you fear is to repeat them over and over again until they are no longer frightening. It could be driving on a motorway, being around dogs or approaching girls in a bar. Everything gets easier with practice and the longer you put it off the worse it will get. You need to put yourself in situations where the pressure is on. Your first couple of attempts are bound be poor. Jimi Hendrix probably wasn't an amazing guitar player the first time he walked out onto a stage. His insane skills came from years and years of practice. In the end, he could walk onto any stage in the world and freestyle to his ecstatic audience without a second thought.

Musicians, sports stars and business people all credit hard work as the core of their success, yet we're all seeking that instant formula that will give us a flat stomach or the Ferrari overnight. The sooner you realize there is no such formula, the more chance you'll have of succeeding. Want to be a music star? Then switch off *The X Factor* and buy a guitar. Want to be an Olympian? Then don't go to the pub on a Monday night, drink five pints and watch the football. Get up at six in the morning and start training before work instead. Hard work is not pretty and it isn't what you want to hear, but it will make things happen for you much quicker. Success starts with that first bit of self-sacrifice, and being brave enough to admit that you want to achieve something big.

One area in which I failed dismally at first but worked hard and learned quickly was public speaking. We had entered a competition with iFoods and made the final three, and I was to give a presentation to a room of investors, media and friends and family. The prize was €10,000, which would have helped tremendously, and I'd never spoken publicly in my life. I paced up and down outside in a cold sweat and repeated in my head all that I had memorized while staring in a mirror for the last week. I imagined the audience sitting there naked and all the other tricks I'd been taught. Sean, my co-founder, calmed me down as I whispered outside about maybe just forgetting it all and doing a runner back to my apartment. My presentation was horrendous and we came second in the competition. We badly needed that €10,000 for the business but we didn't win it because of my poor performance. I had stuttered, missed my lines and lacked confidence. That night I told myself that this sort of public speaking would be essential in my new business career and I'd better get good at it pretty damn fast or I'd be laughed out of every investor meeting.

As it happened, fate intervened to give me an even bigger incentive when we were selected to pitch on the BBC's *Dragons' Den* in front of some of the most successful entrepreneurs in the UK. The show would be seen by a TV audience of 6 million. Sean had submitted the application and we found ourselves with less than a week to prepare.

We practised and practised until we knew the pitch off by heart but nothing could ever prepare you for walking up those stairs and meeting the Dragons face to face. The pitchers aren't allowed to see either the Dragons or the set in advance, so the 'rabbit in the headlights' look most of them wear is genuine. The first couple of minutes were tough but we soon started to engage in a bit of banter and I suddenly relaxed. Sean was looking after the numbers so all I really had to do was try to show our passion for the product. We came very close to getting the €100,000 investment we were after but in the end, because of an issue with the company name (a competitor had one that was almost identical), we didn't get it. As we walked down the stairs empty-handed I heard Deborah Meaden say, 'Wow, they were impressive and they'll do well.'

From that moment on I knew I'd never have to face anything as tough in terms of public speaking. I'd hit the fear head on. I started doing more talks and presentations, and although the standard was still pretty poor I was no longer scared. Consequently, I started to relax and improve. Now I do about fifty public-speaking gigs a year and I stride onto stage often not having looked at my slides or even thought about what I'm going to say. People commend me on my public speaking now, which is such a transformation from my original talk back in the iFoods days.

The more you repeat something and practise it, the more natural it becomes and the smaller the risk of failure grows. If there is shit you want to get done but you either fail or are scared of failing, just practise it over and over again and put yourself in really tough situations.

The most remarkable company in my generation has been Facebook. From one guy on a laptop in his dorm room to a service used by 1.3 billion people and valued at $150 billion within a decade. The world has never seen the likes of it. I've studied their culture from afar for years and with Lauren, my partner in Simply Zesty, I used it to help model the company during the early days. They innovate, they change the world and they do so with a disregard for the past and the way business used to work. When I visited their HQ in Palo Alto the posters on every wall said 'MOVE FAST AND BREAK THINGS'. What that means is don't be scared to fail.

I've never seen a company of that size and scale with such an entrepreneurial culture. They encourage their engineers and management to take risks. Failure is seen by the entire company as laudable. It's why Facebook has ongoing success and keeps re-inventing itself. Other large corporations are happy to focus on the balance sheet and eke out profits to keep shareholders happy. Facebook might strike out ten times before one of their products connects. You'll never hear about the nine failures, but without them the culture to hit the one home run wouldn't exist. An ordinary product would have been created rather than something groundbreaking.

Technology is disrupting every industry, from media to music right through to hardware, and any company unwilling to take risks is not just losing market share but flat out failing. Look at Nokia and BlackBerry, two former behemoths of the phone business who not only ignored the iPhone but wouldn't even acknowledge Apple as a worthy competitor. Within a few years those companies and others like them lost billions in value and have either been subsumed into other larger organizations or had to change their nature radically. In our modern business world maintaining the status quo is rarely good enough and failure to embrace change might even mean the end of your entire business. Just ask the recording companies in the music industry.

The same thing applies on a personal level. Our parents and grandparents were taught that learning a trade or gaining qualifications would ensure a job for life and a decent pension, but the new economic reality has removed those guarantees. We might well expect to have multiple careers, failing often and jumping between various jobs as quickly as the companies we know come and go. The news media provides a classic example of the ground beneath an industry shifting constantly. It is vital that new graduates have a range of skills that span IT, journalism, new media and self-promotion. Smart individuals who are adaptable and willing to change will succeed and get shit done quicker than ever before, but those unwilling to embrace change will very quickly be left behind.

People often compliment me on my business and personal success, but I cringe when they do because I know myself that I'm not especially smart or well equipped to succeed. If I could put it down to one thing it would be that I no longer have a fear of failure. Absolutely zero. I'll try anything and do my best not to fail but I'll also stand up and say that I didn't get it right. I'll say that I failed.

Every success story is littered with failure, and the sooner you learn to embrace it, the better. The good news for you is that the vast majority of people give up at the first sign of failure – they buy Lotto tickets instead of putting their life savings into that killer business idea, or stay rooted to the spot when they should be walking across the bar to talk to someone who's been smiling across for the last twenty minutes. By losing your fear of failure, you will put yourself ahead of the pack. Once you have that trait, you will be nearly unstoppable because you will have conquered the single biggest inhibitor that we all face on a daily basis.

The easiest option is always to say no. To find a reason not to do something. To avoid the risk. If you want to get shit done then learn to not only deal with failure but to welcome it.

3

Influencing people is key to getting meaningful shit done

The first time I cooked for Bill Gates I was standing behind a makeshift barbecue and he asked me about the steaks. 'Where are they from?' he asked. 'They are Wagu beef from Japan,' I said, pinching myself and feeling slightly star-struck. 'Oh you are Irish,' he said. 'Yes, but I'm kinda happier to be out here cooking for you than back in wet Ireland,' I replied. He smiled at my lame joke and moved on to talk to the next chef serving the salad.

I'd had a two-line conversation with the richest man in the world and I bragged about it to my friends and family on Skype that evening. It had made my entire year and I'd have a story to tell in the pub and share with my grand-children for ever.

About six months later I was on another boat cooking for his CEO, Steve Ballmer, when Gates came up on to the deck. I was standing behind a sushi station in a com-pletely different outfit on a different boat in a different part of the world. Gates broke away from the small group of people he was with and wandered over to my station. 'So, what type of sashimi do we have tonight, Irish?' he said. Here was the richest man in the world who had briefly met me once, throwing one word into a sentence that showed he remembered me. I was floored.

The point of this story isn't that I was flattered or that I got to cook for Bill Gates (though that was pretty cool). The point is that Bill Gates used one word to influence me in a positive way. It wasn't even my name – he remembered my nationality, another incredibly important thing to us all.

I've told that story a thousand times. I've used it at conferences and cocktail parties when people ask me what it was like cooking for the rich and famous. I'm convinced that Bill Gates approached me thinking something along the lines of, *I need to influence this little Irish guy because one day he'll be writing a book or speaking at conferences*. It was one of possibly hundreds of interactions he has on a daily basis with all sorts of people, from CEOs to lowly bartenders, but clearly he understands the power of influence.

You don't become the richest man in the world by simply being good at coding and coming up with software used by hundreds of millions of people. You have to influence people to write the code with you, get bank loans, build sales teams and convince your family to give you the time you need to achieve your goals. When we look at very successful people we often have a simplistic view of them and we think that people like Facebook's Mark Zuckerberg are just geeks who got lucky, but that couldn't be further from the truth. Gates might have been a genius programmer in the early days and that was enough to get him started, but to become the richest man in the world, or even the most powerful person in your home town, you need to learn how to influence people. It could be something as simple as remembering their name or driving team members on to a sales target right down to being humble enough to stop and hold a door open for a cleaner when you are the boss of your company.

If the richest man in the world spends time influencing people with small gestures like that we should all probably be doing it too.

I was working on a yacht in Cannes during the film festival when I heard the captain – ex Royal Navy, very posh and proper – telling someone on the other end of the phone that there was no way of getting out to our boat at 3 a.m. The conversation continued and when he hung up he turned to me and said, 'That was Bono and he says could we send in a boat because he wants to sing a few songs at the party.' It seemed Bono had heard we were hosting the best party in Cannes that night and wanted to come over. And he got his way. All rules were broken and a short time later Bono was on board with mic in hand banging out a few tunes with the world's most famous people eating out of his palm. He kissed girls' hands, listened to old boring businessmen attentively and worked the room to perfection.

Bono's interaction with a crowd at a concert is always remarkable, but it is the way that he uses his ability to get people on his side in every other part of his life that is his real skill. I've seen him about a dozen times and he is without doubt hands down the most influential person I have ever encountered. He is mesmeric, and although not everyone's cup of tea he can influence absolutely anybody.

The night he turned up on the boat in Cannes I was finishing up my shift down in the galley and at 7 a.m. I was ready to hit the sack and hand over to the daytime chefs. My mate, an Aussie waiter, came on the radio and said that the party had thinned down but that there were thirty-six people left and they all suddenly had an appetite and wanted to eat before finishing up. I cursed my luck but still had supplies of burgers, nachos, chicken wings and everything else drunk people who are partying like to eat. But my mate walked back into the kitchen and said, 'You are not going to believe this but Bono is up there and we got talking and I told him the chef is Irish. He has convinced everybody that an Irish breakfast is the best thing in the world and they'd like to order thirty-six of them.' *The annoying little bastard*, I thought to myself. I spent the next hour rustling other chefs from bed, defrosting bacon from the freezers and making a giant pot of scrambled eggs. It took me about forty-five minutes but thirty-six people up on the top deck enjoyed a fine Irish breakfast that morning thanks to Bono.

Another time on another boat he sneaked down into the serving area upon hearing one of the girls was mad about U2. Because she wasn't client facing she wouldn't get the chance to see her hero in person despite him being so close. As she stood making a pot of coffee up crept

Bono and placed his hands over her eyes and whispered, 'Guess who?' After nearly having a heart attack she came to her senses and was beaming from ear to ear and had a story to last a lifetime. Bono had just converted another few thousand people by proxy in the same way Bill Gates had.

You don't become rich and famous only because of talent, and I am sure there are hundreds of singers out there who are technically more competent than Bono, but he has probably been influencing people like that since he was a young boy. Is it an accident that Bono was an early investor in Facebook, is friends with all the world's most powerful people, has saved tens of thousands of lives and is rich beyond his wildest dreams? Of course it isn't. Bono is more than a rock star, he is a world-class influencer.

If you want to build a company, a team within a company, or indeed achieve anything significant you are going to have to influence people. You have to bend people to your way of thinking. Convince them to give you their money, their time, their energy or even just their blessing. The guy climbing the mountain is going to have to influence his wife and family to let him do it. Influence his boss to give him time off. Influence some like-minded folk to go with him because a mountain is a lonely place and training on your own is nearly impossible. Along with that he'll need a bit of money too, so sponsors or a bank manager will need to be influenced as well. Influencing people and bringing them round to your way of thinking is the key to getting shit done.

In some ways the word 'influence' carries a lot of negative connotations. Politicians are influential. Bankers are influential. The Church is influential. But I'm talking about something much more basic here, and that is getting people to buy into your way of thinking. It touches on people actually liking you and believing you. You should be working on your own influence all the time.

There are a million ways of influencing people and one of the most simple is to call people by their name. People love the sound of their own name, and if you shout it they'll turn round with a smile on their face. Recognizing someone wins you instant kudos. When we are introduced to a large group of people most of us instantly forget the names we've just been told, yet there is always one genius who seems to remember them all, and it's that person everybody warms to. They've shown that they are smart, care about their fellow humans and instantly have command of the room. Though it wasn't my name but my nationality he recalled, this is the lesson I learned from my second encounter with Bill Gates: if you can show that you remember people you will have them in the palm of your hand.

Influence is not like power or control and it doesn't require underhanded tactics or a strong will. In fact, you can just do it by being nice, being kind and helping people. For example, send a handwritten thank-you card when somebody does something nice for you like passing over a piece of business. This is so much better than sending an email. Writing an email takes seconds and no matter what it says the gesture is quickly forgotten. Although it is a pain in the ass, walking down to a shop, getting a card, picking up a stamp and envelope and taking the time to write a message raises the gesture to an entirely different level.

At one stage we were going through a rough patch at Simply Zesty, losing three big clients in as many days. We were growing too fast and had neglected some of them as we sorted out our growing pains. Losing any more clients could have had such a crippling effect on the business that we might have had to let a couple of staff go or scale down our ambitions. All of us in the management team were scratching our heads. How could we fix it all quickly? None of us had an answer. Then, while I was walking home that night, it struck me to start writing letters. I took out thirty pieces of A4 paper and in my childish scrawl wrote a personal letter to all our clients thanking them for supporting a small Irish start-up, asking them to please bear with us as we grew and telling them they had put a smile on the faces of twenty young Irish people who now had jobs because of them. I sat up until 5 a.m. writing those letters and posted them all myself the next morning. It stopped the rot, and we didn't lose another client for a year after that. If you were a client reading that letter from a young founder thanking you personally, could you ever let that agency go? What would flicker through your head when you went to sign the contract for the next twelve months? Would it be that the work could have been done a bit better, or the handwritten letter you received?

Something else that makes an impact on people is being considerate. Given that our lives are so busy these days, it can be a very hard notion to scale. How do you show a couple of hundred people in your network that you are constantly thinking about them? One thing I do is to send out links to stuff online. I read a lot and I often spot something that might interest somebody else. That article about Amazon, for example, might be useful to my mate Geoff, who runs a large online retailer. It takes me three seconds to copy and paste the link and fire it over. Some sites let you share stuff with the click of a button, and even that simple action shows that I'm thinking about somebody else. That person will remember that. They might even send it on to a couple more people with a note: 'Got this from Niall'. This is the online version of the Bill Gates trick and it helps you scale the influence you have from behind your keyboard.

Another trick is helping people with stuff online. I call it the planting 10,000 seeds technique. Let's use Twitter as an example. Most of us spend our time trying to get the attention of the people with 10,000 or more followers, the so called influencers. I prefer to engage with somebody with ten followers. What you need to do is help anybody you can. What do I mean by help? I mean answering questions. If somebody asks where is a good place to eat out I'll give them a good answer. If they listen to me and have a nice experience they'll always remember me. If somebody is looking for info on social media or marketing I'll jump in and try to help them. People won't thank you for trying to persuade them to visit your website or buy your products but you'll be amazed at just how much you will rise in their estimation when you help them. And when you need assistance in the future you'll be rewarded with an army of people willing to help you.

I can remember two instances of helping people with fewer than a hundred followers on Twitter that led directly to contracts for us at Simply Zesty worth over €100,000. Perhaps the person you help has a sister who is a bank manager, or one of their own followers is an investor. Just remember that while a celebrity might have 50,000 followers, the people you are looking to add to your network, be they lawyers, journalists or business partners, might only have a couple of hundred.

Seeding influence like this won't always generate results within a week, a month or even a quarter. It won't get you hired overnight or gain you loads of customers tomorrow. Helping people and planting 10,000 seeds should simply become a way of life. Wake up every morning asking 'How am I going to help others more than myself today?' and you will find that the opportunities and the network you create will be more powerful than you could ever imagine. I've used online examples here but the same applies in the real world, from holding a door open for somebody to being extra generous with your tipping.

*

Standing by people when they are down is the absolute key to future loyalty and getting people on your side. There was a period when my business partner Lauren was under huge pressure. She was really stretched to her limits and her work was suffering. She rang me shortly before she was due to give a presentation to a group of twenty, saying she wasn't in a position to do it. I didn't know what to do. People had travelled from all across the country to be there.

I went to see her, and arrived to find her extremely concerned that she was letting both me and the business down. I agreed with her, though – it was just one job too many; somehow I'd have to cover for her. It was a pretty tricky morning for me as I bluffed a class on Facebook analytics, a subject I knew very little about, and got through the entire day worried about Lauren and trying to juggle phone calls with clients during breaks. But in business or in life, when your partner is in need you do what is necessary to help them. Lauren had been there for me in the past and it was my turn to reciprocate.

Sheer exhaustion compounded by stress was wearing her out. One night she called me to say she was feeling extremely anxious. I ran up the road in a T-shirt and jeans in the middle of December and met her walking towards me. We went into her house and I sat with her and we chatted until she was feeling calmer and less anxious. After that, Lauren moved everything into my tiny studio apartment, including her smelly cat, and for a while I did both our jobs at Simply Zesty. It was hard to see somebody I cared so much about going through such a bad time. It took her a month to get better physically, and longer to be completely back on form, but thankfully she is now fully recovered.

I did what I had to do for my business partner at the hardest time in her life. I wasn't doing it for selfish reasons, but I benefited from it none the less. Lauren has never forgotten those moments, and when later I had my own battles I didn't even need to go calling – she was just there for me. A good business partner or the people you surround yourself with to get shit done are the sort of people you don't need to go looking for when things go belly up. You just know they're there, 100 per cent committed, and willing to walk through a wall of bullets for you.

Building that sort of loyalty from people around you is tough but essential, and you'll only get it by backing people when they are down and forming a bond with them. It's the reason Sir Alex Ferguson would never publicly criticize his players, no matter how much they were in the wrong. Stand shoulder to shoulder with people, show them that you trust them and pick them up when they are down. You need many different attributes in those around you but one that stands out for me above all others is loyalty. You want it in a wife or husband, a business partner, employees, teammates and anybody else important to you. You'll nearly always get it from family and that is why successful people often surround themselves with family members despite their many other limitations.

In my early twenties, when I thought myself bullet-proof and was hanging around with people full of bravado, I used to think that there were tons of people who had it all. Perfect lives. Great careers. A happy family and not a care in the world. It is only now I've run a couple of businesses and gained some more experience that I realize everybody has issues. Some are bigger than others but people are remarkably good at hiding them. Family members with cancer. The most outgoing upbeat people like myself suffering privately with depression. People battling the bottle. Drugs. Shyness. Disease. Unrealistic expectations. Everyone has their demons, and if you help people conquer them with care and support they'll be loyal to you and help you get shit done.

If you are running a business you can't think of people as numbers. You have to think of them as your brothers and sisters and support them when they are down. You can have a mediocre business by treating people badly and taking them for granted, but if you want to achieve wonderful things and get remarkable shit done then you need to show absolute loyalty to staff, partners and friends. If you do, they'll reward you with the same or more in return, and that will help you get the really big shit done.

Working with my first Michelin-starred chef, Conrad Gallagher, was a terrifying experience. There were twenty staff in an extremely tight area cooking under great pressure. I entered the lions' den voluntarily as I walked in the back door and asked if I could peel potatoes for free just to get an experience of the kitchen. It was the best place to work in town and there were no jobs going but I chanced my arm.

I was eighteen and a boy among men in every sense of the word. It was a world of huge piping-hot stock pots, sharp knives and even sharper tempers, hungover chefs shouting abuse at each other. We worked sixteen-hour days with only Sunday off and it was the equivalent of SAS training for chefs. In my first three months there I saw over fifty chefs come and go. I saw grown men crying and one guy actually run out of the kitchen and jump into his car saying he was never coming back. At the end of every shift I was a broken man both physically and emotionally.

On one especially gruelling day I'd worked through heat, sweat and immense pressure from 6.30 a.m. without a break until one o'clock the next morning. The last hour had been spent polishing the stoves and I was gagging to get out to the late bar to lash five pints into me before closing time at 2 a.m. As I was walking to get changed with blisters on my feet, my brain frazzled and my back aching, one of the especially tough chefs came in with two boxes of tomatoes and told me he'd need a fine dice of those for the morning, a two-hour job at the very least. My heart sank. The chef was French, a language that, unbeknown to anybody in the kitchen, I spoke perfectly after growing up in Belgium. As he and two other senior chefs walked out the door laughing as they headed for the bar I heard him say, 'That will break the little Irish bastard. I don't think we'll be seeing him back tomorrow.' I chopped the tomatoes that night until well into the morning and vowed I'd get the last laugh.

Chefs in the kitchen all had at least seven or eight years' experience and there was a very traditional route to promotion that meant it took three or four years to progress. My progression depended on keeping the head down, working crazy hours and making every piece of food I presented perfect while I endured dogs' abuse from all the older lads. Incidents such as the French chef's tomatoes were regular occurrences. I was right down the back of the kitchen and the only interaction I had with Conrad was when he heard my Northern Irish accent one day and asked whether I was Protestant or Catholic. I answered Catholic and he said that was lucky, because if I'd said Protestant I'd have been fired. I presumed he was joking but you could never really be sure.

As in every restaurant, up at the front of the kitchen – the pass – was where all the action was. That's where the meals were plated and hours of work would come together under Conrad's fierce eye. I saw him throw entire plates of prep in the bin because there was one speck of dirt on a tray and give chefs ferocious criticism. You didn't get near working with Conrad unless you had about ten years' experience and were über-talented. I peeled my veg at the back of the kitchen and grew in confidence but still kept my head down and tried to stay alive.

One day the guy who plated starters was out sick and so was his sidekick who covered for him. I'd worked a little on their section and was asked to help. It was a super-quiet lunch service and there was a bit of joking going on without the usual edge in the kitchen. I realized that the job up front was actually far easier than the gruelling stuff I was doing down the back. That evening Conrad was on the pass with me. I plated a couple of dishes. He was bossing people around and the atmosphere was tense again. Nobody dared answer back and the food getting sent out was magnificent. The kitchen was really humming. I was plating my last starter and as I knew I was in the home straight and had done a good job I suddenly grew in confidence. I still don't know where it came from but as I leaned over to grab some herbs for the last plate Conrad was blocking me doing some main courses. 'Move up, you fat bastard, and stop slowing me down,' I said to him as I grabbed the herbs and gave him a pretend nudge. Everybody else was busy and focused on their own tasks. He gave me a little wry smile and as I headed off that night I wasn't sure if I'd done well or if I'd be getting my head shoved into an oven in the morning.

The next day the guy I'd been covering for returned and I was back on spud-peeling duty. Lunch was quiet. When the pace for dinner picked up Conrad started barking orders. Suddenly he shouted at me, 'Niall, you little Tyrone bastard!' and I think I shat myself a little down the side of my leg. 'Give those potatoes to François; you are up here with me tonight.' From that moment on I was

Conrad's gofer. I fetched herbs, brought him water, went and got him clean aprons and generally took abuse but I had a seat at the very top table, as it were. I'd bypassed years of training with one well-timed cheeky line. Now the journey to being a head chef wasn't as simple as all that – the pressure was immense and the lack of formal training caught me out in later years – but it taught me that even the biggest and most terrifying people can be influenced if you have a bit of neck and pick your moment. A little over two years later, when I was just twenty-one, Conrad made me head chef of one of his restaurants, putting me at the head of a team of eight, many of whom were twice my age.

I never believe people who say that they really don't care what other people think about them. In any case, it's sensible to care. The simple fact is that if you are liked you will end up getting more shit done. The people who are liked very often get picked for promotion over more talented colleagues – which is what happened to me in Conrad Gallagher's kitchen.

There are some simple things that you can do to be more liked. Being thoughtful and nice is one. Sounds simple, but treat people with respect. Listen to them and show that you care and you'll get a lot in return. If you are a boss, hand out a free lunch or let people go home early on a Friday if the sun is shining and the work is slowing up anyway.

One of the biggest mistakes we all make is that we

spend most of our time in attack mode. I see this most of all in cities, where people ignore each other, jostle for position in traffic and snatch stuff from the hands of lowly service staff. Nothing gives you the divine right to treat people like shit. I always make it a point to put some effort into the tiny interactions I have with people when I am out and about. The coffee queue in the morning is a great example of this. I observe people and they usually take out their annoyance at the early hour and the rain and whatever else is bugging them on the person serving them. They bark their orders, grab their change and never utter another word. The bar is set so remarkably low that a simple 'Hello, how are you this morning?' from you to the server will help brighten up their day.

I don't care how late your rent is or who is sick in your family, surely we can all make the simple gesture of being nice to each other. Holding doors open, letting other drivers out or stopping to talk to an old person and giving them two minutes of your day are all simple ways to influence people, plus it makes you feel bloody good about yourself. It doesn't cost much time, money or energy to be nice, and although the payback might not be instant and the next person you meet might be rude back to you the key is rising above it all. There is a way to get ahead that doesn't involve being an asshole.

Don't try *too* hard to be nice, though, or you'll look sycophantic. I'm talking about developing a mindset where you are considerate to everyone you meet because it's a civilized way to behave, not just because it makes you look good. When I hire somebody I can nearly always tell what they are going to be like straight away. Somebody who is loud and pushy during their first week rarely stays long. Sometimes you need to be patient and play the long game. Keep the head down. Earn respect. Nobody is going to get promoted in their first week in the job. Star players don't often put in a match-winning performance in their first game – rather they are consistent over time and help others. Whatever situation you are in, be nice, take your time and above all help everybody you can, because being liked will get you a lot further than not being liked.

I've raised investment three times now. Each time the amount has been €500,000. I've also sold a company for a couple of million. People parting with large sums of money in the hope of making themselves more money is an incredible spectator sport. Human behaviour in the midst of fund-raising rounds is worthy of a David Attenborough documentary: you see every human emotion including greed, joy, fear, hope, despair and anger, and with so much on the line a person's real character reveals itself. And though you may never need to raise capital or sell a company, you will probably buy a house, where similarly high finances are at stake.

Whenever I've raised money I've first prepared a detailed business plan. These tend to be about fifty pages long, full of lofty theory and detailed financial projections that are at best guesswork and at worst downright lies. See, people don't invest in business plans, nor do they invest in ideas, but they invest in people. Walk into any pub and you'll find ten brilliant ideas all with the potential to be billion-dollar businesses. I could download a pretty decent business plan from the internet, edit it up a bit and change some numbers and have something pretty plausible on paper by tomorrow morning. Walmart is just a shop that sells cheap stuff. There had been hundreds of other airlines before Ryanair came along. I'm sure they had business plans as well, but it is the people in them and, crucially, the drive they have that has made those companies what they are today.

Investors' decisions are usually based on how they feel about the people asking for the money. Yes, there's usually a presentation or a couple of meetings and a business plan to thrash out, but the key moment comes when the would-be investor looks the entrepreneurs in the eye and asks, 'Do I want to give these people my money?' Business plans are long forgotten and more often than not the answer is 'no'. Fund-raising is about making people look you in the eye and say yes.

Our biggest deal so far, selling Simply Zesty to UTV, was a classic example of how so much comes down to personal chemistry. Lauren and I had started the company in my spare bedroom in Sandyford with just €10,000 between us. I'd just come off the failure of iFoods and Lauren had been an account executive in a social media agency in the UK and knew nobody in Ireland. We were hardly Fortune 500 material. Through a mixture of hard work, luck and the rising tide of social media we grew our marketing business so that within a couple of years we employed thirty people and had made an impressive name for ourselves. Several people came knocking to buy the business and in mid-2012 we, along with our CEO Ken, decided the time was right to sell.

It took a while to find our buyer. The deal was on and off again numerous times. We whittled down the list of people we wanted to work with and eventually it came down to UTV. Ken and I went to thrash out the terms and it ended in disaster. We left with our tails between our legs and the deal was off. Months of hard work and our dreams were in tatters. Although both sides had advisors – two founders and Ken on ours and goodness knows how many on theirs – somehow we couldn't get it over the line. Stalemate. So I picked up the phone and called their CEO and said I'd like to drive back up and meet him the next day, which was Christmas Eve. The CEO and I sat down in the UTV boardroom and he made me a cup of tea. It was an incredibly formal place, totally unlike Simply Zesty, the kind of place where you expected a flunkey to waft in with a tray of tea and some delicious biscuits. I'd never met the CEO before, and somebody told me later that in thirty years he had never made anybody a drink. He was a wise man who had seen it all and was coming towards the end of his career. He treated me like a gent, asked me some questions about my family, the business and my own ambitions. I answered as best I could and he put me at ease. I decided there and then that we could work with this company and he clearly felt the same way.

Although there were financial terms to be discussed and legal work to be completed that would take another three months, we stood up after a fifteen-minute chat and shook hands on a deal done. Not once did either of us talk about figures or spreadsheets and business plans, because that would be for another day. It reinforced my opinion that people do business with people, not with spreadsheets. I called Ken as I drove back, and as I walked in the door I hugged Lauren and said, 'We have a deal; we've sold our company.' I knew I could take the CEO at his word and that he wouldn't let me down.

You can build a business that has thirty staff, negotiate for months while lawyers do sums and accountants assign values, but at the end of the day it comes down to two people looking each other in the eye, shaking hands and saying, 'Yes, I think this is somebody I can trust and do business with.'

I think people forget when they are trying to raise money, do a deal or sell their company that there has to be something in it for both sides. You can't come to the table thinking, *I am going to screw these guys and get everything I want*. These are your future partners. First you have to like each other and be comfortable around each other. What is written on paper is just a tiny part of the equation.

People do business with other people. No matter how much technology evolves and the world changes, business has always been about influencing other people, just like it was back when the world was run on the spice routes and barter. Rather than working on fictional financial projections for your business, figure out how you can influence the people you need on board. That will be a much better way of getting shit done.

Apart from generally working on being a nicer human being, to achieve your goals you have to become nuanced at manipulating people's emotions and pushing them in certain directions. Sounds underhanded, distasteful and morally suspect – right? Well, the truth is it happens all the time but I'm just putting it down in writing here. Take this book. I want it to be a number-one bestseller and to do that I needed to influence you into buying it. That could mean you have followed one of my blogs. Maybe spotted a couple of my tweets. Heard me in the media. Clicked on an online advert. Liked the cover which was specially designed to attract your attention. Been struck by the catchy title when walking through an airport. Maybe you saw a feature in a newspaper or heard me talking about it on the radio. There are such a wide range of influential tools available that it can be hard to know where to start. When you walk into an average bookshop there are about 10,000 books to choose from. On Amazon there are millions. So why pick up this one? The answer is simple and it applies to nearly every facet of our personal and business lives today: marketing.

I put my heart and soul into writing this book over six months, sitting up late at night racking my brains for great stories and deleting thousands of paragraphs because I just didn't think they were good enough. It was edited to within an inch of its life and I rewrote parts of it at least ten times. The content is massively important but I would say that the content will only equate to 10 per cent of the overall success or failure of this book in terms of sales. Are you really telling me that a bottle of Deep RiverRock bottled water is better than a bottle of Evian water? Or that Carlsberg is better than Heineken? My ass they are. It is all down to marketing.

Start influencing people today to get shit done. Influencing is not manipulating people, and indeed most of it can be done through kindness. You have to be perceptive to other people's needs and you have to stand out from the crowd. Standing out from the crowd does not mean being bossy or being noisy or trying to get attention; it means being kind, fair, thoughtful, hard-working and having longevity. Elon Musk might build great cars and Facebook COO Sheryl Sandberg might have been able to deliver incredible results at Google before getting the job but they didn't and couldn't have done any of that on their own. While being a product visionary is a great trait, you are going to need to learn how to bring people along on the journey with you. To be aware of the needs of others. I'll work myself into the ground and cut my family off while earning feck-all to make my company a success but I'm acutely aware that not everybody else will. People have mortgages, friends they want to see, personal goals to achieve, and you need to be aware of those. If you are selfish and focus only on what you want and try to manipulate people into helping you achieve your goals, you'll fail.

When I was a head chef at twenty-one I used to think that I could win by cooking the best food and being a bit of a cock to everybody else. I thought that I was a one-man show and that no matter what happened I controlled my own destiny. It was only in later years, as I grew up as a man and as a chef, that I realized I had to influence my supplier to want to bring me the best produce and to deliver my goods first in the morning so that I could get a head start over my competitors. When I was young I used to fight with the waiters and scream at them to get the food out quicker but that always backfired as I found them putting in impossible orders to the kitchen. Only when I became friends with the waiters did I realize that they were my best salespeople and they could sell whatever I wanted to the customers. Two pieces of expensive fish left in the fridge that I needed shifting? Talk to the waiter nicely, cook him some dinner and he'd move them for me. I could shout and scream at my staff all I liked but it was only with age that I realized I'd get the best out of them by building their confidence, teaching them new stuff and giving them genuine career prospects while still maintaining their trust. A kitchen is the perfect metaphor for everything we do. On my own I could cook the best meal that anybody had ever tasted but without influencing those who helped get it to the table I'd end up with patchy, inconsistent results at best. By getting everybody on board and being attuned to their needs I was able to produce incredible food and so influence hundreds more people.

Whatever you do, you will only ever achieve so much on your own. If you want to get really meaningful shit done and shoot for the stars you'll need to start influencing people.

4

Life hacks – the keys to getting a lot more shit done

I'm in a cafe in Dublin when my phone pings and the Airbnb app tells me I have a new booking request. It is in two days' time and somebody wants to rent my house for a week. A businessman and his family are coming in from France and he wants somewhere that is not a hotel where they can cook and enjoy the city while he works. I click approve, which means I'll be getting €2,000 hitting my account on the day of his arrival, and I get to work on some quick logistics. I book a professional cleaner to come in and sort the house and iron sheets and put clean towels in the bathrooms. I book my dogs in to stay with a dog sitter and juggle some meetings. (Given my aversion to meetings, I only have one or two to clear and they can be Skyped anyway.) I tell Emma, my business partner, I'll be working remotely for the next six days and then I flick open the Ryanair website to play Ryanair roulette. I call it that because every time I get a booking I look for the cheapest destination on the website, which on this occasion happens to be Oslo. It's €120 return and I have it booked in a matter of minutes. Finally, I fire up Airbnb and find a gorgeous room in the best area and I book it for six days at a price of €300. Within twenty minutes everything is done and I get back to work safe in the knowledge that I am about to get paid to go on holiday.

Two days later I am sitting by the harbour in Oslo with the Nobel Peace Center on one side, a gorgeous fjord on the other, eating local food and drinking a strong coffee. It is eight o'clock and thanks to some TripAdvisor research on the way over I've found that this is the best cafe to work in for the day with free Wi-Fi, good food and plenty of plugs for my laptop. The really good news is that because of the time difference it is only seven back in Ireland and I have a head start on everybody in the office and all our clients. Inspired by the view and my sense of adventure at being in a new country, I have more work done by nine o'clock Irish time than I would in two normal days back home battling traffic and household chores such as putting out the bins and doing my washing. I've paid somebody to do it. Because I use Google apps and instant chat and Skype, and my mobile is running apps like Whatsapp and Viber over Wi-Fi, I'm more connected than I could ever need to be. I chat with people in the office, checking sales targets and plotting our growth with Emma.

After a day of brilliant work and clear thinking I grab an ice cream and sit watching the people of Oslo catching their ferries home in the autumn sun as I admire the city. That evening I go back to what is effectively my own apartment. A quick jog around the city takes me to a hip neighbourhood that I would never have found if I was looking at guide books and sticking to the beaten track and I make my way up there for dinner and to write this chapter of my book. After tweeting that I was in Oslo there are two people who have suggestions of where to get coffee and food and one Irish person who wants to meet up for a drink. I'm behind on my deadline for this chapter so I decide to work on it from the comfort of the back of a lovely tapas bar in the hip area I've found, safe in the knowledge that I am experiencing something cool and new and getting paid into the bargain.

Working remotely is one of the first life hacks I'm going to share with you. I've discovered it because I've never had to work in the confines of an office and spent my early years as a chef, and I genuinely think that over the next couple of decades, as the way we work continues to change, this will become the norm for many industries.

Offices are probably the most inefficient places in the world to conduct business. If I'm asked where and when I get my best work done I'll always say 'On a plane' and 'Late at night or at the weekends'. I don't work well in the office. My day is punctuated by interruptions. People calling me. Emails with problems I have to solve. Losing time commuting. People talking to me when I don't want to talk. Meetings. Meetings about meetings.

If it's obvious that offices are so inefficient, why do employers force people to work in them? I think it is because offices were set up before technology brought us to where we are today. We needed to be in the same room or close to each other physically to get stuff done. That has completely changed now. Physical businesses where you need to meet clients or service industries like coffee shops and butchers will always need bricks and mortar, but why do so many of us still waste time, money and energy travelling to work? Why aren't more employers taking steps to increase productivity, increase worker happiness and improve the environment?

I'd like to see everybody who can work from home doing so one day per week. You would have to be doing something measurable, and work on stuff online or based in the Cloud but in my experience, employees granted the perk of working from home actually increase their productivity rather than skive off because they don't want to lose the privilege. Collaboration in the office is still vital in terms of creativity, culture and getting a team to gel, but shortening the on-site week to four days would do no harm for many businesses. Look at the positives: Employees aren't fatigued by their commute. No money is spent on fares or fuel. Employee satisfaction is increased. Congestion on roads and public transport is reduced.

While it is a great notion and it sounds good in theory, how do you implement this in your own company? Well, the first thing to do is ask. Gather some facts and put a proposal to your boss. Explain the benefits. Maybe take a shorter lunch break and find a way of showing how your productivity would be increased. Whisper it and only use it as a last resort but maybe you could forgo some of your next pay rise. You might think that's a price worth paying for the ability to roll out of bed an hour later, look like shit for the day and get to pick up the kids from school for once. The worst your boss can say is no, and if you play your cards right there is a very good chance they might go for it.

This is another example of asserting your influence over people and bending them to your way of thinking. If remote working has never been tried in your company before, why not be the person to introduce the thought and not only get more shit done but help your company be more efficient? And if you're a boss, you can only win by introducing flexible working conditions. Think of the demands you are placing on your staff by asking them to always be connected to email via their smartphones and working on weekends; this could be a way to give a little bit back. I've calculated that working in this way helps me get at least 40 per cent more work done. Why not see how well it works for you?

In economics and finance, arbitrage is the practice of taking advantage of a price difference between two or more markets. Though it's a technical term it can also be applied to real life. I've only started practising it recently but aim to ramp it up in the coming years to drastically improve my standard of living and to create magical experiences that wouldn't be possible with a conventional lifestyle.

The most obvious way of introducing life arbitrage is to earn money in a country where you can stockpile lots of cash and to then spend most of your time in another country where it costs next to nothing to live. So you could, for example, set up a business that focuses on the Christmas jumper market in a Western country like the UK, earn a large amount of cash in a three-month period and then spend the other nine months of the year living somewhere like Thailand where the cost of really incredible street food is about a euro.

While splitting your time between a couple of countries is probably too radical a step for most people, there are many other ways to arbitrage your life and do amazing things. I've been really lucky to have done it twice in my own life so far. I'd grown sick of cooking in Dublin and staring at the same four kitchen walls every day so I started looking around for opportunities and came up with the idea of doing six months in the French Alps as a head chef. I loved snowboarding, but even though it was one of the most fun sports I'd ever done, and among the best social experiences I'd ever had, my experience of it had been limited to ten weeks of my entire life owing to a combination of the prohibitive cost, lack of holiday time and the absence of local facilities. Getting a job in a ski resort cooking for English tourists in a hotel might not have been the best career move, but I got to spend six months snowboarding and creating one of the most fantastic experiences of my life. I'd leveraged my culinary skills to take me to another part of the world where I could both work and have a great deal of fun.

My other arbitrage moment was when I went to work on billionaires' yachts. I've never seen a quicker way to make money because the pay is pretty good and full board and lodging is provided: you don't even have to worry about buying a drink or doing your laundry. Because you are at sea most of the time it is nearly impossible to spend any money (so long as you don't discover online poker!). I was able to save 90 per cent of my considerable salary and still have a remarkable lifestyle. By the age of twenty-five I was in a position to buy my first apartment outright. More important than the financial reward, however, was the fact that I was travelling the world and seeing incredible places. Most people have to pay to travel, so being paid to see the world is the ultimate life arbitrage.

I did it on boats and in a ski resort, but there are similar opportunities all over the world. All you need is a change of mindset. By combining work with travel you can have remarkable experiences while also earning money. The best of both worlds. If you are a teacher, why not teach kids in Africa? Or the Caribbean? Many professions are as much in demand abroad as at home, and although the pay might not be as good the experiences you have at the weekends will top anything you get up to at the moment on a wet rainy Saturday. They need mechanics in China, dentists in Argentina and nurses in Sydney. Even if you don't have a skill and spend your day doing manual labour on a building site I'm guessing it might be more fun to take a salary cut and do the same job for a year in the sunshine. Finding ways to leverage your skills in a different market is a remarkable way to get shit done.

*

As far as I can see, the average girl starts thinking seriously about getting married at about twenty-six. I think guys do so at about twenty-eight or twenty-nine, and although there are clearly lots of exceptions to this rule it certainly seems to be true of young adults in my part of the world.

Who the hell came up with this convention and why do so many of us stick to it? We're often told that women have a biological clock and their bodies and minds start telling them it is a good idea to have babies, but surely it doesn't have to be like this. I know some people manage to combine success with parenthood, but for too many it marks the phase in life when their dreams end. Not their dreams about having a house and a happy family, but their dreams of riding across America on a motorbike or scuba diving in Bali with dolphins. Dirty nappies, insurance policies and mortgage payments tend to push what are seen as the slightly more frivolous dreams well down the list. Suddenly, before they know it they are thirty-five with three kids and not only are their dreams in tatters but they are struggling under a tsunami of demands for communion dresses, college fees and finance for an extension to match the neighbours'.

Conventional wisdom tells me that as a male I should be well married by now, but I'm hacking my life with a plan to marry at forty, so long as someone will have me. That, I hope, will still give my partner and me more than half our lives together.

It may sound a little clinical, but my point is that I think it's been worth hacking my life to give myself an extra ten or fifteen years during which I don't have the pressures of a family, of being tied to one place or of having another person to consider. I'm hopeful that in those ten years when I am in the prime of my life I can achieve great things and set myself up for a completely different lifestyle in my forties. Maybe when others are mortgaged to the hilt I'll be able to take the time to teach my kids how to sail on a two-month summer holiday without having the pressure of work or a boss emailing me every two minutes. Maybe I'll have the time to cook bread with my wife while we both watch movies all day and plan a remarkable house build that will be featured on *Grand Designs*.

The hack here is that I'm reversing the normal formulaic route that people take to maximize getting shit done and getting it done well. There are, of course, potential pitfalls, such as being hit by a bus on the eve of my fortieth birthday and never knowing the joy of seeing my youngster's first smile. Maybe the other kids will bully my twelve-year-old son because his dad is fifty-five and looks like a granda, but they are risks worth taking. It's an unusual hack, but at thirty-four it has allowed me to do a remarkable amount of stuff that other people only dream of.

I catch about twenty flights a year minimum, and when I do so I'm amazed at the scrum of people who line up at the gate. Seats are usually reserved but most people end up queuing for twenty minutes between the boarding gate and the plane. What I prefer to do is to sit in the departure lounge working on my laptop, reading or making phone calls. I wait not only until every person has handed over their boarding pass but until there are only one or two people left stepping onto the plane. I then stroll down having got twenty minutes of useful shit done and take my seat at leisure. Once aboard the plane, my experience is no different from anybody else's.

Getting on the plane last is part of my attitude to living. For the same reason – making the best use of my time – I do no Christmas shopping before midday on Christmas Eve. Store managers will tell you the 24th is actually the quietest day in December, and if you are really lucky you might even get some bargains from retailers itching to get their sale items out on the shelves. It's the same logic that can help you pick up tickets for the biggest sporting events or rock concerts at a fraction of the cost. Rather than paying over the odds months in advance, stroll up to the stadium five minutes before the event starts and look for a ticket tout. You will always find one with a ticket left over that they are trying to get rid of and you'll be able to get it at face value or even below. No matter how big the event this tactic has always worked for me.

Using this 'last-minute' tactic is very unsettling for most of us. People like to be secure in the knowledge that they have some control over what they are about to do. They like to have the match ticket in their hands, their baggage safely in the overhead compartment or their presents wrapped in early December. Letting go of that security seems terrifying, but the downside really isn't that bad. You might have a couple of mishaps along the way but you'll experience some wonderful events, claw back hours of time and most importantly get a load more shit done by starting to think like this.

I've never really understood why people take their main holidays in the summer. I know that for families there are considerations such as school holidays, but I've always thought the best time to head for the sun is when the weather at home is at its worst. In Dublin the winter days are short and the weather can be pretty grim. On an especially rainy day it feels like it barely gets bright at all and you'll trudge to work before dawn and leave for home after dark. That's the time to go on holiday.

I'm writing these words sitting on a beach in Thailand in December. You might think that's extravagant but the flight was €500, the cost of living here is next to nothing and the sun is always out. When you compare the price to a holiday in a concrete costa during the European summer there certainly isn't much difference. So when people are worrying about frozen windscreens, Christmas traffic jams and party hangovers I can go snorkelling, enjoy a three-hour Thai massage for €20 and then eat some amazing, and amazingly cheap, food. The flipside is that you stay at home while the rest are away, but the summer days are long and often warm, so it isn't the worst prospect in the world. It's another life hack that involves doing the opposite of what the masses do, and it works super well.

Still on the travel theme, how do you get the best possible accommodation? No product has a shorter shelf life than a hotel room. What is on offer – the use of a room for a specific night – can never be sold again. A lost sale cannot be recovered. When I am travelling I never book online. Instead, once I'm at my destination I'll call or visit my chosen hotel and ask for their best deal. The first quote is usually the full rate, or very close to it. That is standard practice. But if you leave it late enough, you'll probably be offered a deal, since any income is better than none. I might say a competitor offered me a room for €80 and they'll magic up a rate of €70. The later you leave it the better deal you will get. It is the ultimate game of brinkmanship, but once you know how to play it the rules are the same in every hotel in the world.

The worst thing that can happen is you'll have to stay up all night and the best thing is you'll save yourself a fortune and get to stay in some of the world's swankiest hotels for next to nothing. I've done this over a hundred times, securing ridiculous rates for palatial accommodation, and only been caught out once, ending up in a room fifty miles away. Ironically, that happened in Dublin.

While I was writing this book I realized I was losing an incredible amount of time to my phone. I'd be sitting in meetings looking at alerts popping up on Facebook, checking emails or monitoring stock price updates. I had become addicted to my smartphone. For the first time in my life I suddenly had this powerful pocket computer that could deliver everything from streaming video to newspapers to weather reports and social networking. I was waking up in the morning and before even rolling over to look outside I was checking the revenue numbers from the previous day in work and what had been happening on the Nikkei overnight. I'd be out for dinner with a friend I hadn't seen in years and rather than fully engaging in our conversation, I'd be checking the score in a Bundesliga match. I realized in 2013 that I was no longer controlling my destiny; instead, my phone had started to control me.

Then, by a strange set of circumstances, my phone was cut off. I was facing a busy couple of days in work and the only way to get it reconnected was to go to the shop in person and sign a contract. A couple of days slipped to a couple of weeks and before I knew it I'd been a month without a phone. My entire way of engaging with the world changed and I went back to interacting with people like I used to. Rather than standing in a lift with my eyes glued to the screen I started talking to people again. I used to be a menace on the roads as I pinged through Whatsapp looking for updates while I snaked through traffic. It suddenly dawned on me that being connected 24/7 wasn't all that great. I used to think it made me massively more efficient but I soon realized that the complete opposite was the case. Instead of attending rugby matches and spending the first half trying to get the perfect Instagram shot to show my friends just how cool I was I actually watched the action and surveyed the faces and emotions in the crowd. I've never been a great man to use the phone for chatting but people trying to call me were simply diverted to the office number. My day stopped being interrupted by people who wanted to get in touch and started being about me doing quality work and focusing on the things that mattered to me.

I'm not going to lie and say it is all plain sailing because I've ended up woefully lost a couple of times without Google Maps when I don't have Wi-Fi coverage and nights out are tricky when you can't pick up the phone and call people you have lost in the same club. But mostly I find that Wi-Fi picks up most of the slack because I do still carry the device (just no longer configured to use as a phone). My house has Wi-Fi, as does the office, so all my apps work and I make good use of my phone when out and about. Perhaps best of all, I'm back to the old days of getting a full day of battery life out of it.

People look at me like I have ten heads when I tell them I don't have a mobile phone. Rather than looking at my Twitter updates when out walking the dogs I actually throw the ball for them to fetch. In meetings I listen to what people have to say and move things along rather than killing time answering emails while the conversation meanders. For the most part living without a phone has allowed me to get a lot more shit done.

I don't know about you but getting healthy stuff into my body is really hard. I've tried simple rules like eating 'five a day' or trying to load up on fish or veggies, but with a busy life it can be hard to do. It's also expensive to eat good food. Who the hell came up for the pricing for sushi, for example? The answer is simple and, despite being a chef for so long, I only figured it out a couple of years ago – juicing. Diets and health fads come and go but nothing is more effective or better in the long run in terms of getting good stuff into your body in a cheap and cost-effective manner.

I'm not talking about those stupid smoothies that are laced with sugar and additives but the sort you make at home. I have a juice every morning and it typically consists of two carrots, half a head of broccoli, a knob of ginger, a handful of spinach, two apples and some celery. Unlike most healthy stuff it is absolutely delicious and takes less than two minutes to make. I would never get that amount of good stuff into my body in a typical day but here you are by eight in the morning with everything you need to give your body a kick start. It also means that unlike most days where you play catch-up trying to eat your five a day you are over the finish line before the day has even started and everything from that moment on is a bonus. There is no downside. The antioxidants kick the shit out of colds and flu. It gives you more of a boost than coffee and it fills you up in a way most breakfast options don't. Buying a shit load of fruit and veg isn't expensive either and a good juicer will cost you about €100 tops.

What I love about this is that it also allows you to have a couple of treats later on in the day. So what if you have a Snickers at four o'clock? Look what went into your body this morning. Rather than juicing being some sort of fad that you take up for a month at New Year or on a crash detox, hack it into your life on a daily basis and you will see the benefits very quickly. After three or four days of juicing you'll notice that your body is responding in a whole new way and that you have a ton of energy that you never had before. I used to have a weak immune system and get a few colds every winter but since I started juicing I haven't had one. It also works for things like hangovers because when you think just how much crap you have put into your body on a twelve-hour session, this is like an instant boost of goodness for the body. Lash one of these into you the next morning and you start the fight-back a lot sooner than you would by having a hamburger or whatever other greasy food makes your traditional hangover cure.

Most of us don't have a spare second to live our lives and get the shit done that we want to. Great plans are often unravelled by having to do menial tasks like accounting, cleaning the house or spending half the day queuing up for a new tax disc. It is the drudgery of daily life that kills our time and ambition to get the really good stuff done. There is a simple solution to this that I discovered in business and now apply to my personal life – outsourcing. Getting other people to do the stuff you don't want to do frees you up to do the stuff you have always dreamed of, like surfing, learning how to dance or picking up a new language.

So what does outsourcing look like? It's getting a cleaner. Paying a professional accountant to do your taxes. Hiring somebody to queue up for you at the motor taxation office.

Your initial reaction is probably that you can't afford to do any of this. You struggle on your salary as it is. I thought the same in my first few start-ups as I spent days learning how to file my tax returns and hours delivering documents in person to save ten euros instead of booking a courier. Our natural instinct is to save pennies wherever we can. Most of us will baulk at the idea of spending a couple of hundred euros on an accountant to file our returns. We'll even laugh at the idea of paying somebody twenty euros to compete a menial task for us like mowing our lawn or taking a trip across town to pick something up. We worry about an extra ten cents on a cup of coffee and drive miles to a cheaper petrol station. Yet when it comes to the big stuff, we are happy to throw the money around – a round of beers in a late bar costing way over the odds? Going over the top on Christmas presents? We'll whip out that credit card quicker than you can say APR.

We simply don't think rationally about our spending. Take tea and coffee, for instance. Most young professionals I see buy two coffee-shop drinks a day at €2.50 a pop. That's about €25 a week or €1,300 annually – about 3 per cent of the average yearly salary of €40,000. Now if I was running a business and you told me that we were going to spend 3 per cent of our revenue on coffee I would scratch that expense and tell employees to find a cheaper option. But we don't run ourselves like businesses.

The point I am getting at is that we need to be more strategic in our spending and spend money where it makes sense and frees us up to do more enjoyable or lucrative stuff. I wake up in the morning and decide what I am going to outsource today. The more shit jobs you can get off your plate, the more time it gives you to do the things that you are really good at. I'm not just talking about fun things either, because for this to work you need to make more money than you are spending on outsourcing. Let's imagine you are a building project manager who earns €300 a day on site. By staying home to do your end-of-year accounts for two days you are losing €600. That's what economists call an 'opportunity cost' – the cost of doing one thing instead of another, which in this case is the cost of not being out there doing what you are best at. By hiring an accountant at €200 you not only get the chance to earn more money working but you also get your accounts done properly and on time with half the stress. The key is using your own skills and what you are good at to either make yourself more money or improve your quality of life. Everything else should be outsourced.

Interestingly, this concept is being taken to the next level online. You can now hire an online assistant in a less-expensive country (say India) who can complete tasks such as booking appointments, conducting research or some of the hundreds of other small jobs you have to do each day. An American company called TaskRabbit takes things further by providing a marketplace for people willing to help out with stuff like this. Need your laundry picked up and dropped home? Somebody will do that for $5. Struggling to get across town to get the car serviced? For $20 somebody will take it for you.

At first glance outsourcing might seem an expensive luxury reserved for the rich and famous, but when you weigh up the opportunity costs and realize that it could more than pay for itself, it becomes an attractive proposition.

Life hacks are about swimming against the current to improve results. For better or worse, I like to think of my life as a start-up business. I look at certain parts of it and think about supply and demand. About how I can get the most bang for my buck without compromising on quality. Too many of us try to save the pennies in the forlorn hope of achieving some fanciful dream. This all goes back to the notion of failure and being comfortable with the possibility that things might not work out exactly as you had planned. So what if I'd ended up in a hotel a hundred kilometres outside Oslo and had to spend six hours on a train? Wouldn't I have had an incredible experience and still have made a few bob?

Life hacking can be applied by anyone, anywhere. When I first moved to Dublin I lived in Blackrock but went to college and worked in the city centre. I quickly became tired of catching the DART and night buses around the city. My days were on average sixteen hours long and I was losing an extra two hours in commuting. I couldn't afford a car and was desperate to find a solution. One day I saw a courier zipping in and out of the lines of traffic on a scooter and I instantly saw the hack that would get me ahead of the game. I bought one the next day and for €2,000 I'd shaved ninety minutes off my daily commute and given myself a valuable extra hour in bed. And every time there was a meeting with a client, rather than taking a forty-minute taxi ride I could spend an extra half-hour at the computer banging out emails while other competitors sat in traffic cursing about being late. Years later when I sold Simply Zesty I still had a scooter, the only difference being that I had upgraded to a fancy €3,000 Vespa.

Wherever you possibly can you must hack your life to turn things in your favour. Seek out the hacks that nobody else sees. It will truly help you to get shit done.

5

Go see the world

When you ask people about their dreams, travel always ranks very high on the list. People mark special life events by making big trips, for example a once-in-a-lifetime honeymoon visit to some exotic location. And when most of us think back on our fondest memories they often involve being abroad. A weekend shopping in New York with family. The trip we took with friends when we graduated from school. The gap year adventure. Although I was never good at school, travelling has given me a great education in making the most constructive use of my time, appreciating life, getting the shit that matters done and gaining a unique perspective on the world. Day-to-day life can zip past in a blur of mundane moments but a foreign trip can leave an indelible print in our brains for the rest of our lives.

Most of us have about twenty days' leave a year with a couple of bank holidays and the festive season thrown in. Because of globalization and the emergence of the internet we can now book a plane ticket from our smartphone with just a couple of clicks while sitting in a restaurant. Travelling has never been so accessible or cheap and we have been afforded opportunities that our grandparents would have killed for. So, if travel is so wonderful and we enjoy it so much, why do we all spend such a pathetically small amount of our time doing it? We say that lack of money and time off are the main reasons for not going travelling but I think the problem is our mindset. We see holidays as something to be enjoyed just once or twice a year and at great expense. If getting shit done is about living your dreams and travel is right up there then we just need to think about approaching it differently.

Life hacks can be applied to travelling, too, and one I often use is to spend long weekends in European cities. All I have to do is take the Friday 'off', which just means working remotely in another city rather than being tied to a desk in the office. I book a couple of months in advance, meaning that I am able to pick up a flight for as little as €100. Most people start with a specific destination in mind and pay the price accordingly but I look for the lowest fare and then plan my weekend trip around that. So in the last couple of years I have ended up in places as diverse as Seville, Oslo, Pisa and Budapest. I make sure the flight leaves after work on a Thursday night and I return late on the Sunday. I use this technique to see up to ten new cities a year no matter how busy I am at work or how rocky my personal finances are.

Justifying it financially is easy. You have two main costs: flights and accommodation. As I've said, the flights are about €100 and if you are extremely frugal you can save that sort of money at home within a week. Using Airbnb means that you can find a high-quality apartment or room for about €40 in most cities and even less if you are willing to go to the outskirts. So typically with flights and accommodation you are looking at a cost of about €220 for a three-day break. Once there, make sure that you don't live like a king and spend as you normally would. I try to find cafes that the locals eat in. I buy fresh fruit from a supermarket for breakfast and live as I would at home. My Friday is typically spent working and because I'm out of the office and in a cafe I have the peace of mind and focus to do a much better job than I would have if I'd stayed in Dublin.

Think about what you would spend at home: €30 on the cinema with unhealthy snacks; impulse buys during the Saturday shop; a night out with friends. All that could easily come to €200 or more. In Europe's less-expensive spots (Serbia, Hungary and Spain, for example) I can actually save money by going away for the weekend. I'll sit in on the Friday night and watch a movie on Netflix, for which I've already paid a subscription. Next day, rather than spending money on a brunch as I would in Dublin I'm out on a rented bike or having a jog round a new city. My €100 Saturday night out with friends is replaced by people-watching with a six pack of beer as the sun goes down. And walking around a beautiful square in a foreign city eating an ice cream and enjoying a new culture is far better than watching the latest blockbuster with a giant tub of popcorn.

As the plane touches down on a Sunday night from whatever destination I've spent the weekend in I always feel a sense of achievement. I come back with new ideas, bursting with energy and a focus that most other people can only dream of bringing into work on a Monday morning.

Travelling isn't just about having fun; it can also help you discover great new ways of doing business that change your whole approach when you return home. You can cherry-pick best practice from all over the world and bring it home with you. When I walked into Facebook's HQ in Palo Alto I suddenly felt alive. As I admired the bicycle racks with high-end racers strapped to the walls, the graffiti-covered boardrooms, the cafes serving free food around the campus, the staff in T-shirts and casual gear, and, of course, those MOVE FAST AND BREAK THINGS posters everywhere, their culture electrified me. There was an almost manic feel to the place with engineers huddled over laptops hacking stuff together and nobody standing still or taking their time doing things. It didn't feel like one of the most valuable companies in the world but rather an extension of the dorm room where it was started. Yes, they had managers and processes in place but the culture that had got them so far had very much been maintained.

Spending a couple of hours on the Facebook campus made a lasting impression on me. We live in a world where we are told we need to work or build a company in a very specific way. Nine-to-five. Wear a suit and dress smart. Lunch is at 12.30. The boss drives everything and we all know who's who in the pecking order. Were it not for travelling I would have been bound to that very rigid way of thinking and would have followed the examples I saw all around me when I was growing up. But because of experiences such as the visit to Facebook I know there are other ways of doing things. For instance, I now know it's smart to allow your staff to bring their dogs to work. We do it in all my companies. Why should people have to wear uncomfortable suits when they don't meet clients? What's wrong with just some simple smart clothes rather than having to fork out hundreds of euros on something that is expensive to maintain and downright uncomfortable? Look at the industries in which a suit and tie are almost compulsory – banking, politics, stockbroking – and you'll see that the suit is hardly a guarantee of trustworthiness. Indeed, some of the richest, most successful and happiest people I've met dress comfortably and for themselves. I dress in jeans, a hoodie and trainers because those clothes make me feel comfortable, are much quicker to put on and are easier to care for, and because I am being myself and not trying to be somebody else I get way more shit done.

I focus closely on the culture within my companies. The wonderful culture I've managed to create is a direct result of travelling; seeing Facebook; sitting in cafes and meeting other start-ups in Berlin; being at tech conferences in New York and San Francisco. People have to spend forty or so hours a week at work so you might as well make it fun. If people love what they do, love their surroundings and are happy in their work they'll be far more efficient and you'll end up making a great deal more money in the long run.

Travel also has a remarkable way of putting things into perspective. Throughout my travels I have seen a side of the world that makes me appreciate every second I'm alive. We've all been to countries worse off than our own but we tend to forget quite quickly how bad things are for others when we are back in our cars giving out about rush-hour traffic. I once worked on a boat where we attended the New Orleans Jazz Festival shortly after the city had been devastated by Hurricane Katrina. As we docked and walked around the city it really didn't seem all that bad. Apart from a couple of closed restaurants, the streets looked like those in every other American city I'd ever been in and I was starting to think that the media had probably made a bigger deal out of the tragedy than it warranted. The next day, back on board, word went round that the owner wanted all the crew to go up in the chopper for a ten-minute spin around the city. We were all excited at the unusual jolly but it was only when we got up there that it became apparent why the owner wanted us to take that trip. As we banked over the outlying areas of the city the destruction the hurricane had wrought became apparent. It wasn't just the odd house that had been destroyed: entire neighbourhoods had simply been flattened and washed away. One car park had been moved a few miles by the floods and a couple of hundred cars lay piled up like Lego bricks. From the air you could clearly see where the floods had breached the defences and blocks upon blocks of houses had just vanished, leaving only a small amount of rubble scattered here and there. As we landed back on our boat nobody said a word. Afterwards I told myself I'd never worry about a parking ticket, a flat tyre or an overdue bill ever again. People had been living normal lives one day only to see everything they'd built over generations simply vanish, with their friends and family dying around them.

I've had the same emotions when travelling around Cuba for three weeks or spending a couple of months in Zimbabwe as a youngster. Although both countries had great tourist appeal you didn't have to look far to see the abject poverty and grief that living under a dictator brings. People who couldn't afford rice. Mothers begging for water for their children. People jumping for joy when you gave them a couple of dollars. We always say that the Irish are super hospitable and friendly but we are a shower of grumpy so-and-sos when you put us beside the wonderful people in those countries. Strip away all the material goods we have and all you are left with is the human spirit and people with nothing to trade but their kindness. It shows you a truly remarkable side of humanity.

I'm so happy that my parents ensured that I saw as much of the world as I possibly could, for I've learned much more from travelling than I ever did at school. I think parents everywhere should spend less time worrying about their children's formal education and simply take them to as many places as possible. It doesn't need to be halfway across the world or on an enormous budget. A child who learns French in school for three years will understand less about the language than one who has lived with a non-English-speaking family in France for two weeks. It is amazing how smart we all are and how quickly we adapt to tricky situations when abroad. If more people focused on travel we'd have far less racism and xenophobia than we do today.

Poverty and disaster can teach you a lot, but you can also learn a great deal by seeing how the other half lives. On my travels I have seen people spending money as if it were toxic. Working on yachts showed me the insanity that can result when people get super rich. One week an incredibly wealthy American businessman hired the boat I was on at a cost of €80,000 for the week. He was a bit of a party boy and spent most of the week with groups of girls dancing to techno music up on the top deck. On the last night of the charter he invited the crew to take the night off and go with him to a nightclub in St Tropez, the European party capital. It's a tiny little fishing port in the south of France that during August is full of super yachts, rich Russians and global celebrities like P. Diddy and Donatella Versace jumping from party to party. We all cleaned down our work stations and headed down to Les Caves du Roy. I've never felt as important in my life as the red rope was pulled back and we passed a queue of about fifty people whispering and trying to identify this group of young celebrities. As the manager ushered us to our private table our host ordered a huge bottle of champagne called a Jeroboam. I looked at the drinks menu and saw that a bottle of beer was €15. I didn't look any further and just felt glad I wouldn't be picking up the tab.

Despite it being some of the finest champagne you could get your hands on our host told us to mix it with Red Bull. *Sure, fuck it*, I thought as I carried on. Within an hour we were hammered and we all started dancing on the tables and up on the podiums. As the night progressed I found myself on a podium with the champagne-and-Red-Bull concoction in my hand and busting some horrendous moves. I looked to my right to see possibly the biggest celebrity in the club, Paris Hilton, dancing beside me on her own podium.

As I pinched myself the night was coming to a close and the celebs had all flittered away to their yachts and even more exclusive parties. Our host asked for the bill and although I was practically slurring my words at this stage I did manage to catch a glimpse of it. Although we'd been in the club for no more than a couple of hours, the eight of us had managed to rack up a bill equivalent to the price of a small family car: €11,500. As we all staggered back to the boat I remember the host saying to his buddies, 'It wasn't that great a night and it'll be good to get some sleep and take it easy for once.'

The next morning I woke up with what is without doubt the worst hangover I've ever had. As I walked into the hot kitchen on that rocking boat and started to cook,

I wanted to die. I've never puked before or since, but as I rushed to the rail and spilled my guts out into the open sea all I could think about was how much had been spent to get me into this state. A 'not-great night' had cost more than most people earn in months. More than people in Third World countries earn in years. As a student, I learned to live on five or ten euros a day. You get by. Yet here was a guy who had so much money that he was able to leave a €1,000 tip to the beautiful girls serving us.

It turns out that being stinking rich and drinking over €10,000 worth of champagne in a night really isn't any more fun than having a couple of pints in the local bar with your mates. We all think that having that amount of money brings eternal happiness but it doesn't. I could count at least 500 nights where I had more fun than I did that night in St Tropez. Drinking expensive booze and dancing with A-list celebrities might be an amazing story to tell your friends but I found the whole scene false, with very little genuine craic and no one really enjoying themselves. They were all too busy looking at themselves in the mirrors.

To travel well you need to set goals. How many times have you done something that made you feel amazing and resolved to do it more often? Except you don't, because unless you give yourself a goal to reach, that resolution is soon forgotten. It's the same with travel. Having good goals in place is essential. Once a year write down five or six places that you are going to visit during the coming twelve months. Don't just make a general resolution at New Year to 'travel more' because this, alongside your other resolutions, will all be forgotten by mid-January. Instead, on the eve of your birthday, take a piece of paper and a pen (because it's too easy to erase a digital goal when you don't achieve it) and write down your age and the countries you're going to visit in the next year as an absolute minimum. I'll typically have six or seven trips that I want to take.

Put that list somewhere prominent, such as beside the bathroom mirror or on your bedside table. This ramps up the pressure on yourself. Visiting six countries in a year means travelling on average every couple of months, so you'll always be just back from a trip, planning one or about to leave for somewhere new. This makes it much harder for you to just go out on a Friday night and lose an entire weekend. There is only one way out of this now, and that is ripping up the list and throwing it in the bin — which would make the whole thing pointless.

A great way to make sure you don't back out is to book the flight, which will usually be the most expensive part of the trip. Most people like to plan an itinerary, research hotels and read reviews before buying a plane ticket. In other words there is a hell of a lot of procrastination that goes on before all the stars are aligned and the button is clicked. I work the other way round. I pick a cool city to go to, find the cheapest flight and book it straight away. Once you have reserved your seat, cancelling will lose you money so you're unlikely to do it. With the flight arranged, everything else will fall into place and you'll always have plenty of time to get the rest of your stuff lined up. Be impulsive and whip that credit card out when you are suffering from a bad hangover, super busy with work or just watching TV.

These simple techniques will help you travel more and get really cool stuff done. My goals become more ambitious every year and the focused approach always pays off. If possible, add an activity into the trip so that you are doing multiple shit in one holiday. At the moment I'm planning to cycle a stage of the Tour de France during the summer, which will not only take me somewhere new but also get me fit and achieve a crazy goal. You can play tennis in Spain, learn to kayak in Finland or take dance classes in Geneva. Teaming up other activities with travel is no more expensive than doing them at home and it creates incredible memories.

I've encountered hundreds of people in all walks of life who have taken a year out to do nothing but travel and to the very last person they all say it was the most incredible experience ever. One of the things they would be thinking about on their deathbed. An incredible journey that they all would love to make again. But 99 per cent of them never do.

The problem with travelling in this way is that it is seen as a once-in-a-lifetime experience. Why? It certainly isn't for financial reasons, because although many people choose to take out a bank loan, tap up their parents or save money in advance you actually need remarkably little money to travel. When I decided to head off at twenty-three, I went to Australia with the flight paid for and €2,000 in my pocket. Not a penny more. It meant I had to work for the first three months I was in Melbourne to save the money to fund the next part of my trip, but it was working in perfect sunshine while swimming in the evening and experiencing a new part of the world in my time off. I also managed to get a job at the Australian Grand Prix circuit, which put me at the heart of an incredible event while getting paid for it.

So you don't have to have a small fortune saved up to go to the other side of the world, and you don't need to have mad skills either, because if you are willing to work on a building site or pick fruit there will always be a job for you. Hack your year together by working in countries that pay well and then travelling and relaxing in countries where it costs next to nothing to live. As an example you could spend three months working in a bar in Canada, saving up your tips, exploring a new city and working your ass off. A simple flight to Thailand and you could be living like a king for a few dollars a day eating street food and staying in a hut that costs a couple of bucks a night.

The other limitation people put on themselves is to travel for just a year. Why? If something is such fun, why not do it for a couple of years? Why not extend the fun and create an even more magical time in your life? If you work while travelling you can extend your time abroad and get more done. Some of the happiest people I know have travelled not for one year in their twenties but made it a way of life, criss-crossing the world for six or seven years. When they settle down in one country at the age of thirty they are no longer promising themselves 'I'll travel when the kids leave school' or 'We'll see the world when we retire'.

If travelling for a year without any responsibility or a paying job is a step too far, there are other ways to live your dreams and create amazing memories. Possibly the best of all is to spend time in another country and get paid for doing so. The six months I spent working in a hotel in the French Alps cooking for English tourists on tiny budgets was never going to win me any awards, but it did allow me to indulge my love of snowboarding. Look for similar opportunities to earn money while experiencing something new. Your horizon should be limited only by your own ambition.

There are people who make vast sums of money by spotting trends on their travels and bringing them back to their own country. In Dublin we are about eighteen months behind the biggest trends in New York and six behind London. Take burritos, which spread across New York as the latest must-have foodie trend a few years ago. I ate them from vans on the streets and rued the fact that there weren't any in Dublin. Burrito bars soon started popping up in the UK and sure enough they eventually arrived in Ireland. This sort of thing happens across all industries and if you can spot the opportunities you can get remarkable shit done in your own country.

Entrepreneurs who sit in a room with a blank sheet of paper trying to dream up the next big idea might do better simply to travel abroad, see what is happening in more popular, trendier countries and bring that 'innovation' back home. Wars fought over spices or the trade in wild animals across the Roman Empire show people's historical love of the exotic. Travel has always been at the heart of innovation and entrepreneurship, be it Italians bringing pizza to the USA or the rise of the humble Irish pub in nearly every city in the world. You need have no misgivings about copying other people because even companies like Apple or Facebook cherry-pick the best ideas from elsewhere. One of my heroes, the great chef Marco Pierre White, once said, 'You can't invent new recipes or dishes until somebody invents new ingredients.' Nearly everything has been done before, but by being open to new ideas on your travels and taking them to new places you need rely only on your own execution rather than any great innovation.

I've been focusing on my own passions here, which are food and technology, but this sort of thinking can be applied to any industry. A hairdresser seeing that all the big trends were coming out of LA might combine a holiday in California with some research into what is working at the leading edge of the industry and will soon be heading across the Atlantic. Get ahead of the curve. Because people in other countries aren't competing with you they'll be far more likely to share information and even trade secrets. You'll never know unless you ask. Whatever industry you work in, be it gambling, footwear or antiques, there is bound to be a place that leads it, just like Silicon Valley leads tech or LA leads the movie business. You can only learn so much online, in books and through theory and the best way to get shit done is to travel and learn from the best in your field.

6

In business – and in life – it's all about selling

I've always been really good at getting into nightclubs. It doesn't matter if it is the fanciest high-end club in Monaco or trying to sneak a late drink in down on Leeson Street in Dublin. Walking up to a nightclub door and getting in is basically a type of sales job. With sales you need to get into the other person's head and figure out what they want. When a group of eight fairly drunk guys approaches a nightclub door the bouncer will be sensing trouble. The last thing he wants to be doing is cleaning up puke, splitting up a fight or turfing people out for being abusive to other customers. Going up to him like most people do and trying to protest that you are not drunk and cracking crap jokes is never going to help your cause and you'll be quickly moved on. What you need to do is give him the answers he wants. I'd typically say, 'Listen, we've had a few drinks after work and the lads are in good form but we all work together and are just here for some craic and to meet some girls.' By acknowledging what he already knows you have him straight on to the back foot. As he stands there thinking, you simply follow up with 'Listen, I'm sober and their manager in work and I'll make sure they are all well behaved.' You've given him all the answers that he wants to hear and made the decision for him. The key is keeping eye contact and making him believe you. That's selling. Do it well and you'll have gotten your friends into a night-club and completed Mission: Impossible.

Getting into nightclubs doesn't sound like much of a skill but it is one I have always related to sales. And sales is crucial to getting shit done, whether in life or in business. People think that in order to be a success in business you have to be good at things like corporate governance, managing systems and HR, but the simple truth is that if you have sales covered you are laughing.

If you ever go through a big financial deal, like closing a large contract or selling your business, there is usually a lot of pain involved. Shadow boxing. When we were discussing the sale of Simply Zesty to UTV it dragged on for months. To the outside world and to our staff it was business as usual but behind the scenes a dozen or so people knew that the company was for sale. UTV was one of five parties who initially expressed interest and we went with them. We entered a process called due diligence that involved them poring over every facet of the business from managed accounts to staff contracts. I stayed out of it as Ken, our CEO, and their commercial guy tried to close the deal. Thrashing out the terms dragged on for months. As anybody going through fund-raising or selling a business will tell you, this is one of the most stressful periods you could ever imagine.

After expressing initial interest it was time to do a final deal and Ken and I headed to Belfast with a mixture of adrenalin, excitement and tension running through our veins. In Chapter 3, I told you how well that went – or didn't: we tabled our demands and after about ninety seconds' chat UTV's commercial guy said the deal was off. We'd blown it. Everything we had worked for over the last few years had turned to shit.

Ken and I didn't talk to each other as we drove home because we both knew we had made a complete balls of it. We'd been too greedy. Too cocky. As we drove down the motorway to Dublin I thought to myself, *I have one last shot at this and I'm going to have to do it on my own.* What happens with big deals is that the decision makers shadow box for ages and avoid each other. Only when they get into the one room and look each other in the eye can the deal be done. Accountants, advisors and all sorts of other people can tidy stuff up but until the main partners shake hands they are just bits of paper and notional projections that people are talking about. This is equally true for somebody buying a second-hand car, a house or a large multinational company. As you know, I asked for another meeting that I'd attend myself and drove back up the motorway the very next day.

When the CEO of UTV walked into their boardroom on Christmas Eve, made me a drink and brought out that piece of paper I knew it was the deal I had to accept. It wasn't the best deal we could have got but it was the deal that everybody wanted to do. Although every minute detail had been discussed for ages it essentially now came down to two people in a room. It still took another couple of months from that handshake to the money hitting our account, but at that moment, the deal was done.

Doing business is all about handshakes and looking people in the eye and making sure you are both on the same page. I find the same in sales, be it for a €500 package on PR slides or a €100,000 food order for a billionaire's party. If I'm spending a lot of money, and especially if it is my own money, I want to be able to look at the person I'm giving it to and see that they are legit and that there is a face behind the promise. No matter how complicated lawyers and accountants make things, people do sales with each other and not with pieces of paper or spreadsheets. Being able to put your best foot forward in sales situations, be they work related or personal, is one of the most important skills you'll ever learn. Even if you're not a natural salesperson, there are some simple techniques you can master that will help you get shit done.

All across the world there are colleges charging people for MBAs, masters degrees and all sorts of other fancy qualifications. Up to €100,000 for the high-end ones isn't unusual. But one thing they can't teach is selling. Don't get me wrong, there are great courses that can improve how you sell, but the vast majority of the best salespeople I know are self-taught. Hustlers. People who just won't take no for an answer.

I've seen this with some of the richest and most successful people in the world and I first heard it when listening to a talk given by Irish billionaire Denis O'Brien to a group of schoolchildren learning about entrepreneurship. He explained that although he had much success he was nothing more than a salesman. All the smart people were behind him, working on the stuff that he wasn't good at, but he was the guy out at the front, selling. From his early days in business to where he was at the time it had always been about selling. I couldn't agree more and I see it in people who have been successful in all walks of life. I know a few dozen business people who are great at what they do. Some are meticulous when it comes to the detail. Some are fantastic with people and can get the best out of their teams. But every single one of them is brilliant at sales. I'm not just talking about picking up the phone (although most are brilliant at that as well), but, simply put, they could sell anything to anybody. Sell the idea of leaving a happy job to come and work for them. Sell the idea of working all weekend to get a project completed on time. People who are brilliant at business or brilliant at life tend to be salespeople first and foremost and all other skills come after that. When I look at Jeff Bezos or Richard Branson I see people who are primarily fantastic at selling.

The greatest salesperson of recent times was Steve Jobs. He was talented at a bunch of stuff from developing product to marketing right through to spotting trends, but his one trait that stood head and shoulders above all the others was his simple ability to sell. To learn everything that there is to know about selling, go online and watch his videos unveiling various iPhones. Let's not forget that this was a product category – mobile phones – that Apple was at least a decade late getting into and was expected to be a niche player. Jobs would organize the events with ferocious secrecy, with nobody outside his inner circle knowing what he was about to reveal. He would stride onstage and with brilliant delivery introduce feature after feature that would blow people away. What was always most remarkable for me was the fact that all these features already existed somewhere else. He would never reveal anything earth shattering but he would have his audience hanging on his every word. He was so good that reporters would immediately start behaving like groupies at a concert and people would line up round the block for days just to touch the device when it went on sale.

Jobs is a great example of a wonderful salesman but he is only one man and it is the effect he had on others that showed me the power of sales. He turned reporters into salespeople. He turned consumers into evangelists as they touched the product and begged others to buy it too.

The beauty of today's business environment is that technology, globalization and social media have completely levelled the playing field. In the past, the only way to reach a global audience was a TV campaign costing tens of millions of dollars, but Facebook, Twitter, Google and LinkedIn now have some of the most targeted advertising in the world and you can start getting your message across with just a couple of clicks. Something we used over and over again in Simply Zesty to get coverage for our tiny brand was viral videos. Whenever the agency got slightly quiet and we were struggling to attract new work I'd summon a team of our best people to create a piece of content that would get us noticed far and wide in the hope that it would attract new work. The costs were minimal because we had all the skills in-house. At the start of 2012 we were in a new-business lull so I called five of our best employees together. The brief was simple – get us a million views on YouTube by Friday on one video and raise the profile of the agency. I always find that with creatives and talented folk you are better off letting them go away and get on with it themselves. Don't impose your own will or stupid ideas on them because they are the talent.

So off went the guys and they targeted an international media event that was coming up, the launch of iOS7 – the new operating system for Apple's iPhone. They mocked up what it might look like and created an animated video. Ninety seconds of hard work that showed off their own and the agency's skills. Next we shared it with some publications we knew and sat back and waited for the video to do its work. The timing couldn't really have been better, with speculation around the event starting to take hold. The video got 1.8 million views and was featured on over 400 online publications including *Forbes*, the *Guardian* and *TechCrunch*. The biggest analysts on Wall Street used it as a barometer to help gauge what a new operating system could do for Apple's stock. Apple blogs read by millions of fans debated the video and we got several emails from Apple's own staff commending it.

We went from a position of having no work to having more than we could handle. We began to charge a ridiculous premium on the video work we started producing as a result. One piece of creativity that had been no more than a figment in the imagination of one workgroup had become a global sensation. Our website had never been busier, phone calls came in from all over the world and everybody felt good about themselves. This sort of viral marketing just wasn't possible a decade ago but now a tiny agency in Dublin was being debated on Wall Street and in Silicon Valley. This is now happening to businesses on a daily basis. It doesn't matter if you are a shoe shop in Berlin or a restaurant in Chicago because the possibilities are endless. The only thing that should limit you when it comes to marketing your business and opening up your sales pipeline is your imagination.

I spend a lot of time investing in start-ups, advising them and generally doing anything I can to give them a leg up. In my opinion the main reason the vast majority of them fail is insufficient focus on sales. I learned this valuable lesson in my first business, iFoods, where we had tons of traction, lots of users and enough hype to easily turn a profit but we simply failed to sell anything. We fell into the same old mistake that most start-ups do, which is to think that 'if you build it they will come' and the money will just start flowing thereafter. It didn't.

The big mistake the vast majority of start-ups make is to think that by focusing on nothing but their product, or maybe their marketing, they will just magic up the sales. Since the failure of iFoods, the very first thing I always focus on is sales and the first question I ask any founder or employee at a start-up is 'How do you make money?' Given that most people are in business to make money it is surprising just how flustered people get when you ask that question. They throw out a swathe of possible routes towards monetization further down the road but they are often more interested in raising money from investors or the design of their new business cards.

Sales solve nearly all problems. The last two businesses I've had have been sales focused. When it came to raising €500,000 of investment we had a bunch of cool slides illustrating stats, growth and the team, but both times we secured investment because of one slide – revenue growth. Nothing gets investors more excited than making money and you'll find them keen to get in on the action if they see a graph showing revenue increasing really quickly.

Just as sales interest investors, they tend to solve lots of other problems within a business. You can always fix your broken HR process or customer service but there is no way for a business to fail faster than not having any sales. Especially a start-up. For businesses that have borrowed to get going, having no sales can be especially dangerous. I often walk into businesses that are struggling with sales and burning through the cash with only months left to survive. What always amazes me is the fact that the management team or founders will often be huddled around a computer trying to decide what's wrong with the website or app. They'll be having creative sessions trying to figure out how to attract more visitors or what shade of grey the new logo will be. The 're-design' is often the biggest hope of turning a business round that I hear thrown out by desperate founders. When you are in that situation somebody needs to shout, 'Stop messing around here, chaps, and start selling. Forget about polishing the edges of your product and hoping your latest video is going to go viral and attract millions of users and increase sales. Make a few sales yourselves instead.' Amazingly, when I say that to people they take offence and often completely ignore the advice. The problem with selling is that it involves picking up the phone or walking into a room and asking somebody to buy your product or service. That isn't easy and invites failure. That is why so many people put it off.

On the flipside of this, the world is absolutely littered with horrendous products and services that people are already buying. The reason people are buying them is not because the companies behind them are great innovators or because their logo has the right Pantone colour but because they have motivated, hungry sales teams who know how to get people to pay for stuff. Can you really tell me, for example, that Salesforce is the best customer relationships management company in the world? Does Microsoft make the best software in the world? Does L'Oréal make the best beauty products? The answer to all of those questions might be yes, but I'd prefer to say that those are examples of companies who know how to sell you stuff. Big companies don't often happen organically and have all their sales fall into their laps. If you are a business of any size you need to learn how to sell if you want to get the biggest shit done. It isn't easy but it is essential.

If you want to achieve anything when it comes to sales you need to master two key elements: building a pipeline and networking. Sales manuals and training will teach you a million other tricks but without these two pillars you won't stand a chance. Building a pipeline is the first step and it involves finding as many leads as you possibly can. For those not familiar with sales jargon I should explain that all the leads go into an imaginary 'funnel' from which they will either be converted into sales or not. Leads not yet followed up are in the pipeline. Most businesses will have a good idea of the percentage of their leads that result in sales and you can make a reasonable guess at monthly revenue by looking at the leads you have. If a business has a 10 per cent conversion rate and generates a hundred leads a month, each potentially worth €1,000, then projected monthly revenue is 100 x €1,000 x 10% = €10,000. It won't always be 100 per cent accurate, but over time you'll be able to evaluate your future earnings just by looking at the leads in your pipeline.

The big problems arise when you don't have any pipeline. It's no good closing 10 per cent of your leads if you don't have any leads to start with. Getting the leads into the top of that funnel is a vital job. Depending on your business, you could source leads from any number of places including Google Ads, direct marketing, speaking engagements, marketing stunts or even through TV advertising. Once you have leads, closing them is often easy enough, but the best businesses know exactly how to generate them and measure their conversion very accurately.

One of the most effective ways to drive sales and get leads into your pipeline is through networking. Everybody has a network, from friends and family through to college buddies and previous workmates. I talk later in the book about building up your online network but much of the business that is done today is between people who know each other personally. People within each other's networks. The stereotype is a couple of men on the golf course enjoying a game and making a deal. That certainly happens, but in today's changed business environment the opportunities to network are legion. It could be the couple attending a dinner party at a friend's house. It could be an industry event where delegates mingle and swap business cards or it could even be somebody who plays on your basketball team.

Most people go looking for sales within their immediate network, but good networking is much more subtle than that. Examples would be an introduction from a good friend who gets you a sales opportunity that would otherwise have been impossible, or helping out other people who might reciprocate with an order somewhere down the line. The more you network and the more efficient you are at it the more leads will fall into your lap. The key is not to shout about your business from the rooftops but instead to listen to other people and help them more than you help yourself. There is nothing more powerful than a favour owed, and having hundreds of people owing you favours will ram your funnel full of new leads that you can add to your pipeline and convert further down the road.

This book is a classic example of what sales should be about. I knew that writing it would be a massive challenge but I believed it would succeed not because of my writing ability but because I was good at selling. I'd go as far as saying that the content of this book might contribute only 20 per cent of its eventual success. From the moment I wrote the first word of the first chapter I was already thinking about sales and the simple fact that I needed to persuade thousands of people I don't know that they have to pick up the book. Just think about how many books are out there on the shelves of shops, libraries and Amazon's warehouse. How do I shift 10,000 copies or get to number one in the bestseller lists? If I simply release it and do a bit of PR I might sell 1,000 copies to people I know – my network and a few who follow me online, but that would hardly be good enough. Equally, I'm no Richard Branson or Roman Abramovich, so my name on the cover won't get people flocking to buy. My unique selling point and differentiator is always going to be my sales pitch.

Selling is the art of getting people to part with their money even though they had no intention of doing so before they saw your product. In some industries a sales cycle could take up to a year; in others it is a two-second snap decision at the point of purchase. I've come up with an extensive range of ways to get this book into your hands. The most obvious is that it is being published by Penguin and they will make sure it is stocked in book-shops around the world. The cover was designed to grab your attention if you see it in a shop window. The title is the same. Who doesn't want to get shit done? The blurb is as short and snappy as can be and written with as many hooks as possible to entice you to buy the book and get the full picture.

I've also been building online communities on Twitter, LinkedIn and Facebook. I've been at that for seven years but I ramped up the engagement in the last six months, knowing that this book was coming. I've connected with every journalist in the land online, helped people with their questions, accepted every invitation I've been sent and generally been super helpful and promoted other people's stuff. I haven't looked for one thing in return but that was all done with the intention of having a huge engaged user base by the time I came to sell my own book. I've tried to create a body of people on the ground who effectively become my sales force. People telling their friends. Others hitting the share button on Facebook. Others retweeting the click to purchase it the second it comes out online.

Offline sales and marketing are just as important in my mind. I'm not talking about massive billboards or other intrusive advertising but rather building a community and connecting with people personally. During the last eight months I've spoken at over fifty events around the country and accepted invitations from anybody who would give me a mic to stand in front of an audience, even if it was as few as twenty people. There is no better way to get people on your side than standing in front of them talking. I've driven hundreds of miles after work in the middle of winter just to give a talk. I've given advice to young entrepreneurs on business, to students on careers, to foodies about social media and I've generally put myself out there. And I never once charged for my time. I'm not going to say it was easy, but I was building another powerful sales channel.

Another key tool is getting the people selling your book to buy into the product they are selling. For example, I'd like every bookshop in the country to stock my book. The reality is that I'm not going to be able to talk to or meet every bookshop owner, most of whom will never have heard of me and for whom my book is just one of thousands on their shelves. But I have been trying to connect with as many of them as possible. Those I've met range from independent bookstore owners to the largest booksellers in the country. I've engaged with them on Twitter. I spoke at the annual Irish Booksellers' Association conference and tried to build as many relationships as possible within an industry that until very recently I knew nothing about. My hope is that my new contacts can help me sell more copies of my book, perhaps by giving it a more prominent position in their shops or by suggesting it to customers looking for recommendations. No bookseller will do that for me unless I know them and can effectively sell my book to them. It's just another channel, but hopefully by meeting them and showing that I care about their business they'll help me sell more books.

These are only a tiny proportion of the techniques I am using to sell this book. I've devised a comprehensive sales plan that features over a hundred clear actions for me to complete. People need to see something three or four times before they connect with it and make the decision to buy. I don't want to leave the sales of this book to chance and I want to make sure I give it every opportunity to succeed. You should think about your business or whatever you want to achieve in the exact same way. You don't just put a book on a shelf and hope for it to sell. For every *Fifty Shades* or Harry Potter there are tens of thousands of books that gather dust, selling only a couple of copies. If the content is good enough and word-of-mouth approval starts kicking in then you open up new levels of sales, but the first step is all about selling and making sure you get enough leads into the pipeline to make it a success with people who have never heard of you.

If you don't have the nerve to pick up the phone or to meet clients and start selling then you are probably not going to be a great success in business. If you don't have a sales mentality, or the ability to acquire one, then you'd better make sure you surround yourself with people who do, or find a business partner who knows how to sell. If you don't, there are plenty out there who will wedge their foot in the door and sell their stuff ahead of you.

I don't actually like selling. I hate driving out to industrial estates begging people to spend their money. There is nothing worse than walking into the office at nine in the morning and having to cold call somebody who has absolutely no interest in speaking to you and being told to eff off (albeit more politely). I also hate going to networking events and explaining to people how my business works and why it could help them. Of course, I'd rather be in the office with the dogs at my feet and a nice coffee in my hand, having a laugh with the team as we watch the sales flow in online. Sadly, the world doesn't work like that and you always have to force yourself to do the things that you hate doing if you want to be a success and get shit done.

You can probably think of a few products and services that sell themselves, and whose suppliers don't have to think like this, but they are a tiny minority. The rest of us, both in business and in our personal lives, need to learn how to sell, and how to fail to sell. How to accept nine refusals in a row before getting that one yes. Selling will break your spirit at times and you'll feel like giving up, but mastering the art of sales is an absolute must if you want to get shit done. Once you start selling your product, running the other parts of a business becomes a hell of a lot easier.

*

Speaking of selling yourself in your personal life, fear of failure and coping with knockbacks, sales skills are also crucial when it comes to dating. In romance, just as in business, some people will be lucky enough to have an amazing product (an attractive face, a great figure, a sparkling personality) that sells itself, but the vast majority of us have to make a bit more effort. Successful dating means convincing someone to come round to your way of thinking and buy into you. That could be because of the way you dress, your sense of humour or just because you're nice and considerate.

Good businesses focus on their strengths: the things they are good at and their best selling points. For companies like Apple it is their design. With banks it is the security they offer. As a businessman, I am terrible at spreadsheets and accountancy, so trying to convince investors, business partners and staff to buy into my mathematical prowess just won't work. I am good at getting people motivated, selling and marketing, so I spend every second I can trying to improve those skills. Approaching somebody in business and acting the financial genius would end in failure because I wouldn't be confident in what I was selling.

Dating is similar. Think about what you are good at and what are your biggest selling points. It could be anything from your job to the car you drive through to the charity work you do. People have different tastes and you need to identify the traits you have that the person you're trying to impress will like most. Your strong points. Think long and hard about your unique selling point and focus on nothing but that and making it even better. If you are a brilliant dancer then spend your time on the dance floor. On the other hand, if all your friends tell you that you are a great comedian, then don't spend your time in nightclubs shouting at people who can't hear you.

Just like all sales, successful dating follows on from not being afraid to fail. How many times has that dream girl walked past you on the morning commute or the Adonis in the corner spent the night checking you out, but your fear of failure has prevented you from trying to take it further? Remember, failure is never as bad as you think. Sure, girls will tell you to piss off if the only time you're brave enough to talk to them is when you are hammered and staggering, but so would you if somebody approached you in that way. If instead you simply walk over at the start of the evening and introduce yourself, you'll be surprised at how friendly and open people are. It might still be a rejection, but at least you won't spend the next few days wondering.

Selling is hard. It's not easy to convince a company or an individual you've only just met to take a punt on you. In business, that means parting with hard-earned cash. The good news is that once you have won that first sale, getting a customer to spend more is usually far easier. Up-selling is a key tool in terms of generating revenue and making yourself or your company more successful. Take the pricing structure in McDonald's. When you walk in, you've already made a choice to buy a meal and the price you saw advertised might have been a major factor. When you get to the counter, though, you'll see a bunch of options that give you a bigger meal for a marginal additional outlay. Chances are, you'll decide to spend a bit more than you'd planned. Up-selling happens all over the world in every industry and it is essential in terms of growing your business.

The key is to look after your clients and make them very happy with what you are selling them in the first place. If you're an online retailer like Amazon and you provide an efficient service delivering books and DVDs, then people will be happy to buy a wider range of products in the future. As Amazon also demonstrates, you might also be able to sell more books simply by improving your recommendation algorithms and showing people more stuff they like. The key to selling more stuff is to sell it to people who are already buying from you and the relationship you have with an individual or a company is another key factor.

For the first two years of Simply Zesty we just worked our asses off and produced great work. A couple of times, despite getting astounding results and servicing the client brilliantly, we lost them to another agency. This always miffed me, especially when I found out we had lost the business because the client 'had a relationship with somebody else'. At first I doubled down trying to do even better work but it soon dawned on me that there are a lot of times when the best work doesn't always get rewarded, especially in the highly fickle world of agencies.

Although I was at first entirely against corporate enter-taining and sending gifts to people I soon realized these were far more effective than doing great work alone. A sad thing to accept, but a harsh reality: up-selling to people you already have great relationships with is the best way to grow quickly. See, many clients are working in nine-to-five jobs earning a set salary and not that bothered about the overall success of their own company. Work for them isn't necessarily the terrific roller coaster of fun that it is for you as a business owner or somebody trying to engin-eer more sales. Entertaining takes a great deal of time and I actually find it much harder than 'real' work, but taking a client to a gig, buying them a meal or playing a round of golf with them really works. It's a perk they wouldn't nor-mally have and it gets them out of the office for half a day. It took me a while to get into that way of thinking but once I did I saw contracts being renewed in record time, people sending us more business and our company win-ning work that would have been impossible otherwise. A simple round of golf costing a couple of hundred euros was often much more effective than preparing incredible work and killing ourselves on a pitch to a client.

Some of you probably already know you are good at sell-ing. Some of you will have had lemonade stalls outside your house as a kid, selling to neighbours, or have started businesses in college trying to make some extra money by selling whatever you could get your hands on. However, the vast majority of people on this planet are not good at sales. You can try to improve lots of other things such as how you deliver work, the way you comb your hair or your accountancy skills, but if you don't know how to sell you are never going to get much shit done.

In Simply Zesty I was the sales guy. I didn't really have a clue about social media myself but put me in a room with people and I could sell them anything from fifty euros' worth of Facebook ads to a €300,000 multi-platform campaign. Getting the sales is one thing, though; delivering on them quite another. I was massively lucky that I had Lauren on my side to run the delivery side of the business and later Ken as CEO to make sure what I sold could be delivered. Many good salespeople need somebody following them with a broom to sweep up all the bullshit they promise in meetings. Good salespeople don't tend to be brilliant at process (although some are). Lauren and I often talk about the success of Simply Zesty and we both know that neither of us could have made it work without the other. If I'd been running it on my own we'd have gained all the biggest clients in the country but they'd have left after a couple of months and never come back because the stuff I promised would never have been delivered. On the other hand, Lauren on her own would have been sitting in the office ready to deliver the most incredible work but with no one to buy it.

If you are great at sales I suggest you find somebody to complement your own skills so as you can keep selling and doing what you are really good at. If you aren't good at sales and know that you will never improve I'd suggest you find somebody who is. Without such synergy, your business will probably fail.

So in both your personal life and your business you need sales skills to get shit done. I've laid out the basics here, and you can certainly learn stuff online and from any number of great resources, but you need to understand that it all boils down to asking somebody a simple question: would they like to buy what you are selling? Most people will say no. That is the reality of life. If, however, you have the courage, persistence and drive to keep on asking despite all the refusals, then you have the ability to get remarkable shit done.

7

Stop being your own worst enemy

One year on from selling Simply Zesty I woke up one Sunday morning at 6.15 a.m. I'd been partying for three days and I had the fear and the shakes and a banging headache. I checked my phone to make sure I hadn't made a disgrace of myself on social media before blacking out the night before, but the shakes were so bad I couldn't really hold the phone straight. I knew the solution. I managed to make it to the fridge and pulled out a half-bottle of red wine. I sat it on the table in my office and fired up the computer. Obviously, I wasn't going to be drinking the wine at that hour of the day but I thought I'd have it on standby for later. I lasted until 6.20 and poured myself a glass. The bottle was finished by half past.

Over the course of the day I drank three bottles of red wine, a bottle of vodka and twelve beers. I locked the doors in the office that adjoins my house and ignored the phone and two different groups of friends who called over to see me. By about two o'clock I'd broken up with my girlfriend, who I was absolutely mad about, and smoked about thirty cigarettes. After five hours' sleep I woke up again, tried to patch it up with the girl only to hear her bawling her eyes out and headed to a late bar in town. The only thing that could sort me out at that level of a hangover was a triple gin and tonic and I knocked back five of them in quick succession. On the third one I glimpsed myself in the mirror and thought about the people I'd been hurting. I said to myself that was it. Never again.

It's amazing how effectively you can hide something as major as alcoholism. I'd been at it for years and made a few attempts to give up. Twice I succeeded – once for six months and once for a year. I wasn't someone who drank every day but I binged at weekends. I'd always be the last guy standing. The guy buying the shots. Wanting to go on drinking somewhere else. Organizing the house party. Drinking didn't really interfere with my work because I built a lifestyle that worked around it. Late nights. Working in the pub. Having a few beers at home and working until three in the morning. Never accepting any meetings before 12 a.m. because although I'd be first in the office I was never operating at peak capacity. I always told myself that as long as I was working hard the drinking wasn't a problem. Sure, didn't Ernest Hemingway lash pints into him when writing some of his best work? It's funny the random things you use to justify your drinking.

We were just days away from selling Simply Zesty when I fell off the wagon again. All the legal documents had been signed and the press releases had been drafted. I had €400 in my bank account and a credit card that had €1,200 left before maxing out. I wasn't broke in any sense and had no personal debt, but the figure on the documents said I was going to be getting €546,780 transferred into my account on Monday morning. It was actually sitting in the lawyers' account. The deal was done. This was the build-up to selling a business – something I had dreamed of my entire adult life – and here I was at thirty-two about to achieve it. Although I didn't know it, the tension was building up inside me and I was like a pressure cooker waiting to explode.

Frustrated at the pace of the deal, I decided to head off for a week working across Eastern Europe. I jumped on trains and worked from cafes. I bobbed along, working away, but I noticed something funny in Prague as I admired a big tray of creamy pints going past and started thinking about having one. I'd been off the booze for a good eight months and things were going awesome. Most people would think of having a pint in a situation like that as a celebration and I talked myself into that way of thinking as I moved across the continent. By the time I got to Berlin, and with only thirty-six hours until the deal was to be signed, I was gasping for a pint. In hindsight, it had nothing to do with celebrating. I was trying to escape as usual. I was terrified and something weird somewhere inside me wanted to screw it all up. The self-destruct button was about to be hit. With me the self-destruct button can be hit remarkably quickly and it takes only a matter of hours to jeopardize a lifetime's work.

So I had a little 'celebratory' beer in an expensive Japanese restaurant. *Just a couple*, I thought. So I had a couple and left. I probably would have found somewhere else to drink anyway, but just fifty yards from the hotel a girl

asked me for a light. I found myself asking her for a cigarette and before I knew it I'd been invited into a press
launch attended by a hundred female journalists. As if
that wasn't temptation enough, there was a free bar. *Fuck
me*, I thought, *the stars really are aligning here for me.*

The rest, as always, was a blur but the last thing I
remember was holding court in a hotel lobby bar where I
was forcing people to drink shots. Needless to say they
were curious as to why a guy was travelling on his own in
Berlin. Before I knew it ten journalists were being treated
to the full story of me selling my business and how it was
a big hush-hush deal that nobody could hear about. I
woke up the next morning with a rather nice Dutch lady
beside me and beer bottles all across the room. I couldn't
remember the last two hours of the night. My thought
process was blurry but it started with . . . *Fuck, I've missed
my flight.* Then I started thinking about the deal and telling
the journalists all about it. *Fuck!* Then inevitably my next
thought was getting more beer into me. My new friend
was quickly dispatched and away to a cafe I went with my
laptop and a serious headache.

Luckily, the story had a happy ending. I told everybody
at home I was having a great time relaxing in Berlin and
re-scheduled my flights. The journalists were more interested in covering fashion and probably thought I was
talking shite. I headed back to Dublin and we announced
the sale of the company. And if you look closely enough
at the pictures from the sale you'll see a pasty look in my
eyes and the signs of a two-day mini-bender.

I probably knew the gig was up drinking-wise on a trip to the US with a hundred Irish entrepreneurs in the summer of 2013. I hadn't really been hitting it that hard over the previous year but it was one final sharp blast that sealed it for me. The six-day trip had started modestly enough and after a few beers on the first two nights I'd gone to bed at a respectable hour. These were the top entrepreneurs in the country on a very formal trip so I was probably watching myself, wary of my previous form. On the third night I got dragged to a student bar on the campus of the University of Notre Dame in South Bend, Indiana and the whole thing unravelled there. Shots and drinking until the early hours meant I missed the bus to the airport the next morning for our chartered plane to New York. There were no other flights that day so in my drunken state I flagged down a car and sped across town, meeting the plane in the nick of time. I got a round of applause and although there were only ten people sneaking in a beer before the flight I made sure I was one of them. 'Take the edge off it,' I told myself. After two more beers on the plane we banked over New York and got the most spectacular view of the city. I remember thinking I'd have two more beers back at the hotel and sleep it off. I was pleased I had learned my lesson by now and was smarter with age. I'd finally turned the corner.

In the next three days I got so drunk that on the last morning I woke up to find I'd lost two phones, my passport, all my bank cards and only had a €20 note in my pocket. My mini bar was completely empty after a party in my room the night before and cigarette butts littered the couch in the Waldorf Astoria. As I walked down to reception I was once again greeted with the news that the bus had left for a quick lunch in the Porterhouse Bar before going to the airport. Although I had nothing with me aside from the clothes I was wearing and my €20 note, I had three hours before the flight so wasn't too worried. I changed my euros into dollars and grabbed a cab to the Porterhouse, where one of the lads would sort me out with cash and I'd figure out how to get home. I even checked to see if thirty bucks would get me there. It would, just about, said the cabbie. After a twenty-minute ride I walked into the Porterhouse and asked where the party was only to be told there wasn't one. 'Could it be the other Porterhouse on Wall Street that you want, sir?' It was.

As I walked downtown with no money, no bank cards and the hangover from hell, the sun came out. *Here I am, a thirty-three-year-old man, and drink has done this to me in just three short days*, I thought. No money, no spare clothes, no passport and no way of getting in contact with the people I was with. Despite being in the worst spot possible and making a fool of myself, I looked up at the sky and smiled. *I've done it*, I thought. *I've hit rock bottom and I've done it in style. I'm never going to drink again.*

My first mission was to get a cabbie to take me downtown. Some of the travelling group had the contacts to sort me and could lend me some money. Try getting a cab in New York with no money. Not easy. In a mad two-hour scramble I managed to get a document that would allow me to leave the country (thanks to the Irish consulate), a taxi fare to the airport and even some deodorant. I arrived at JFK just in time to get the plane home. As I settled into my seat at the back I felt the fear so badly that I started to shake. This was the fear of a three-day bender and running around a city lost for half a morning. I asked a girl who'd been with me on the trip to lend me twenty euros because I'd no money at all. I ordered two small bottles of wine and threw them into me in less than five minutes. That took the edge off it. Mid-flight I perked up a little bit, and even managed a few laughs, but as we landed back in Dublin I knew this level of drinking couldn't go on much longer. Lauren had often said to me, 'If you keep on doing this you'll kill yourself,' and for the first time I knew she was right.

Looking back, I can see I was showing the signs of being an alcoholic as early as sixteen, but like most young people I was having way too much fun in my teens and twenties, with plenty of people up to the same stuff, to ever worry about my boozing. I'd been seriously useful at football and most sports up until about sixteen, but then I discovered alcohol, smokes and women and that was the end of that. Perhaps because my parents' divorce coincided with my fourteenth birthday when I was first discovering the drink, I embraced it with an extra level of gusto.

Most people who know me will be shocked by these stories. I've told five or six people about my drinking and

I always get the same reaction: 'Sure, how could you be an alcoholic?' Don't I have a house? Haven't I sold a business? And don't I drive a nice car and seem happy?

That is the problem with alcoholism – most people just don't understand it, especially in Ireland, a country where life is dominated by booze. It took me many years to admit it, but my name is Niall Harbison and I am an alcoholic. I've got quite a lot of shit done in my short life but I've done that in spite of drinking and not because of it. If I put my mind to most things I can be pretty decent at them, from travelling the world to selling businesses, but alcohol is never far away. It's like a dark character on my shoulder, always egging me on and telling me to give it another lash. I believe I could have sold a business by twenty-five or created a €100-million empire were it not for booze. Booze has made me take the wrong decisions so many times and held me back from achieving my true potential. We all have these sorts of inhibitors, no matter how small and insignificant we think they are, and the quicker you address them or at least become aware of them the quicker you will get more shit done.

While the hacks and tricks in this book are great to get the small day-to-day things ticked off, many of us have powerful inhibitors that hold us back from achieving the really big stuff. Booze is my big inhibitor. It probably sounds like a really bad one but you have to play the hand you have been dealt. You could be petrified of risk. Your family could have pushed you into a career you loathe. You might have a partner who puts you down and doesn't share your ambition. You might be trapped in negative equity. Maybe you are a gambler. Maybe you blow all your money on shopping.

Our inhibitors have lots of different ways of tripping us up and are always there, waiting for the chance to get in and cut the legs from under you. It could be getting super drunk on a date because you are so nervous and messing it all up or not speaking up in a meeting where the golden opportunity was there for you because you were paralysed with fear.

The good news is that there is a way to tackle these inhibitors, and even though it is the toughest thing you'll ever do, the pay-off is immense, enabling you to lead a remarkable life and achieve insane goals. To address your inhibitors you have to follow three simple steps:

1. Identify what it is that is holding you back.
2. Write it down on a piece of paper.
3. Tell somebody what your inhibitor is and how you will tackle it.

The first one is actually pretty easy. We are remarkably good at burying our own inhibitors and I did so with booze for close to fifteen years. The chances are you are doing something similar. Your inhibitors might not be as severe as mine but I absolutely guarantee you have them; if you didn't you'd have achieved all your dreams by now. Once you start thinking about it properly it shouldn't really take you much longer than a week to figure this out.

It isn't going to be easy but you need to go for a long walk, find some space and decide what your inhibitors are. Do you hate your job? Want to be a dancer? Are you secretly gay? Are you obsessed with money? Scared of what your friends would think if you failed? Whatever they are (and there could be a couple of them), you first of all need to admit them to yourself.

The next step is fairly easy but also very significant. Take a piece of paper and in as few words as possible write down your inhibitor(s) with a large marker. You'll be able to nail it fairly easily in five or six words. *I am an alcoholic. I hate my marriage.* Whatever it is, be short and to the point. This is a hugely symbolic step and you won't believe the weight that shifts from your shoulders as you finally admit to yourself what it is that has been holding you back for so long.

You'll probably need a couple of weeks or months to let what you have admitted to yourself sink in. Admitting you have a problem is one thing but starting to address it is something completely different. Just sit with the thought. Carry it with you to work, on holidays or on the commute in the mornings. Digest it.

The third and probably the hardest step is admitting it to somebody else. Find a really good friend or a family member, somebody that you feel very comfortable with, and take them somewhere you are happy and at ease. If you have to, you can break the ice by saying that you have been reading this book and thinking about life. Then just tell them what you wrote. I'm not saying this is going to be easy because it took me a good decade to do this with my own inhibitors, but an admission to somebody else is a major step you need to take. You'll continue to feel the weight being lifted off your shoulders and things will only improve from here. This is only a three-step plan and you'll have to carry on from here on your own, but trust me you'll figure that out. Facing your inhibitors is the first step to removing them completely. Once you have done that you just won't believe how much shit you will get done.

As if booze wasn't a big enough inhibitor I have a second one. I suffer from depression. I have done for about fifteen years, although it has only been diagnosed for the last three. I used to put it down to being tired, hungover, annoyed with work or just having a tough time with business or relationships. When you're depressed, sometimes you can't even summon the energy to get out of bed. It is a fog that invades every aspect of your life. I'll often go months without the slightest problem and then it will hit me out of nowhere, debilitate me completely and force me straight into bed.

When in a depressive phase, you go a really dark place. A place that is nearly impossible to imagine for a person who has never suffered from mental illness. I ignore phone calls. My dogs, whom I love dearly, start annoying me. I get edgy. I sometimes walk down the street thinking people are hiding round corners waiting to attack me. The only place I can find comfort is my own house. With the doors locked. With a pillow over my head and the curtains closed. It usually hits me at the most random times: sitting in a meeting with staff having a laugh or during a family meal. I've become accustomed to having a bunch of excuses ready for when the fog does descend and I'm hit by a wave of depression. I've had an asthma attack. A family member is sick. I'm burned out and suffering from exhaustion. I've been clamped. The list goes on. Sometimes it might only strike for a couple of hours and I'm back to normal but other times it means I lose up to a week of my life stuck in bed, unable to think clearly and struggling to summon the energy to put on my socks. A week during which simple chores like going to buy water from the shop become testing challenges.

It is the biggest obstacle I have ever faced in my life and I'm extremely lucky that I have other attributes that help balance it, including a positive attitude towards business and travel and so on.

Depression is one of the hardest things to deal with for a number of reasons. First is the stigma attached to it. Even though it is far from unusual, and can be caused by something as simple as a chemical imbalance in the brain that is easily fixed, nobody ever wants to say they have something wrong with their head. In Ireland a remarkable one in four people will suffer from depression in their life-time, yet it remains one of the most taboo subjects for people to talk about openly. I don't have any problem admitting to it because I have my own business and I'm lucky enough to be charting my own course in life. I take tablets that keep me grand most of the time. I'd really love to get my depression fixed, and I'm working hard on it, but I couldn't give two shits if people know I am depressed at times. I don't know if I'd be so blasé about telling my employers or work colleagues if I had a full-time job to hold down with a wife and family depending on my money for the mortgage repayments.

I am extremely lucky that I am so determined, because as I lie there with the pillow over my head I use every ounce of my strength to will the thing away. I eat healthy food, I drink juice and I meditate. I'll never let it beat me. I could see how somebody with less willpower and tougher personal circumstances could let it beat them and slip to an even darker place. I've never considered suicide but I understand completely how some people reach a place where they can see no way of living through the fog any longer.

I hate suffering from depression. I spent over a decade being mortified by it and keeping it to myself and hiding it with booze and excuses. I still can't decide if suffering from depression helps me get shit done or hinders me. On the one hand I am bedridden for a week, unable to do much apart from email people, but on the other, when I am healthy I am so determined to make amends that I get an insane amount of work done. I don't want to waste a second because I don't know how long I have before it all goes dark again. I want to get more shit done, though, so I'm hoping I can beat it. I feel great right now writing this, but I know I could walk out the door and be hit with another bout and back in bed feeling sorry for myself.

I know there are millions of people out there who haven't sought help and are suffering in silence, not wanting to admit what is eating away at them. Again, it's all rooted in our fear of failure. Who wants to admit to their family and friends that they have failed at the simple task of keeping their brain healthy? Not many. If one person reading this book seeks help for the first time as a result the entire effort of writing it will have been worthwhile.

Weed is absolutely brilliant and can help you be very creative and inspired and engage with people in new and meaningful ways. I gave it up a few years ago, but only because I wanted to protect my health. If it weren't for the effect on my lungs I'd still be smoking it today. It provides a wonderful escape from the pressures of life and I just don't buy into the idea of it being a gateway drug. Prosecuting users is a scandalous waste of resources. What damage am I doing to society if I roll up a joint in the comfort of my home and unwind after a fourteen-hour day? What harm is there in something organic that can make me more creative and has such a calming effect? (Have you ever heard the term 'stoned brawl'?) Meanwhile, large multinational supermarkets sell crates of beer as loss-leaders, causing people to fight in the street, piss in gardens and clog up our medical system.

Although I tried other drugs a few times in my early twenties, I was never really that excited by them. I'm glad I satisfied my curiosity by trying coke and E, and I won't lie and say that it wasn't fun at the time. What I've found, though, is that people who regularly do drugs are boring. They are desperately trying to escape something and not uttering a word of sense to anybody who doesn't also happen to be high. Everyone I ever met whom I thought was unbelievable fun while on drugs turned out to be the biggest losers or most boring people when sober.

If you're not careful, your surroundings can dictate your drug use. Drugs are everywhere in restaurant kitchens and I'm happy to say I only went down that route a handful of times in those years. The reason they are popular in kitchens is that groups of young men (usually) working in horrendous conditions under massive pressure are more in need of a release than most. I remember once seeing a chef doing coke off the back of a knife during service. I was too busy fighting my own corner to pay much attention, though.

A normal day in a high-level kitchen could start with three painkillers and a coffee for breakfast to ease the night before. You'd probably have five coffees before lunchtime and a Red Bull during service to get you going. Lunch would be a sandwich or a few chips if you were lucky but food wasn't really a priority. After cleaning down during the lunch break if things were quiet early in the week we might get an hour or two off in the afternoon. We'd duck straight into the nearest pub and neck a couple of pints. You'd usually be able to get through three or four, no matter how little time you had, and you could feel yourself buzzing after the night before. Back in the kitchen for dinner, and if you were smart you'd feed some of the waiters and then they'd happily bring you coffees all night to keep you going. You'd probably have another few painkillers as the service kicked off and you had to focus, washed down by another Red Bull. Come the end of the night you'd be straight on the beers and everybody would have a good five pints chased by a few double vodkas in a nightclub before going home and repeating it all the next day.

At the time I told myself I needed all that to keep me going and that everybody else was doing it, but the truth was it was inhibiting me from reaching my true potential in a professional kitchen. By twenty-two I was absolutely burned out, which is a fate that hits many chefs at such a young age. The body can cope with that sort of abuse pretty well when young, but not for much longer. While coffee, booze, headache tablets and drugs help you get shit done in the short term they certainly don't in the long run. And as for more serious drugs, never mind about them stopping you getting more shit done – the simple fact is they can be lethal.

While there are lots of chemical and natural ways to escape your life and stop you getting shit done, the biggest inhibitor of all is the only one that you can control, and that is yourself. To be more precise, it is your own willpower. Willpower is something we associate with sticking to a diet or not having that final shot in the bar that tips you over the edge. Those are good examples, but we are all going to be hit-and-miss at that sort of stuff.

Willpower for me starts with the thousand choices you have to make on a daily basis when trying to achieve your dreams. What you must do is single out one large task and figure out how you are going to make a series of decisions that will give you the unshakeable willpower to get it done. Let's take the example of buying a house before you are thirty. It is a dream most of us fail to achieve and we think it simply isn't realistic. But you can achieve anything if you have enough willpower. Buying a house might take you two years, but if you start doing the right things immediately after reading this paragraph you'll have a much better chance of getting there. It means saving as much money as you can. That means not having a meal out with friends tomorrow night and cooking at home instead. It means watching a movie at home instead of going to the cinema. It means taking a second job for one night a week. It means sitting up late at night researching how to do the conveyancing. It means walking to work two mornings a week and leaving the car at home. Achieving one colossal goal starts with making thousands of smaller decisions on a daily basis and making the right one as often as you can.

Everybody can learn to have willpower by doing it in small steps. So if you think you have a thousand decisions to make a day, just try to change fifty or so if you can. The small things like walking past a shop when you feel like going in and buying something to cheer you up. Reading for twenty minutes before bed instead of watching TV. Improving your willpower isn't an all-or-nothing situation, where you either gets loads of shit done or get nothing done at all. You can nibble away at the edges and take the first steps. Start small, for instance by leaving a chocolate in the box or putting five minutes more effort into your day at work and achieving something that could marginally increase your chances of a promotion. If you try to change everything overnight you are only setting yourself up for failure. Think how rarely New Year's resolutions or crash diets work. Make yourself conscious of the thousand decisions a day that matter and start making some of them a little better; you'll be surprised just how quickly your willpower will improve and you will begin to get better shit done.

I've spoken at length in this book about technology and how it can help us achieve everything from working remotely to networking, right through to helping us get more sales for our business. I also think it has the potential to have an incredibly negative effect on the amount of stuff we get done. Everywhere I go these days I see people who are woefully addicted to technology and who are letting it ruin their productivity, social lives and the amount they get done.

Facebook is a classic example. Most Facebookers use it daily, spending at least twenty minutes there and constantly checking for updates. Because it is on our mobile phones and invading our work life it is very easy for the lines between online time, social activities and work to become blurred. Facebook themselves have a vast team of people whose job it is to keep you on the site (or, as they call it, 'sticky'). The addictive little red pings from notifications are meant to distract you from what you are doing. Twitter is exactly the same and there are hundreds of apps out there which are all determined to suck as much of your time into them as possible.

I stopped using Facebook at the end of 2013 and deactivated my account, simply because it was taking up too much of my time and inhibiting me from doing real work and getting shit done. Quite the opposite from worrying about my privacy or considering it a bad service, I shut it down because it was just too good. Facebook had completely cracked the code of attracting me into the site a hundred-plus times per day, be it to read the news, see updates from friends, listen to music or interact with colleagues via private groups. When I took a step back I realized that all the value in me being there belonged to Facebook. I was interacting with people I hadn't seen in person for a couple of years and getting distracted by content that wasn't adding anything to my life. Instead of me going online and watching videos about business or learning new stuff, my news feed constantly had me clicking on pictures of dogs or lists of funny photos. I decided that I needed to cut it out to become more productive. Since I've left the service I've felt absolutely no void in my life. It may only be twenty or thirty minutes per day that I've recovered, but added up over a year the value of that recovered time far outweighs the benefit of the social interactions I was having there.

Because we carry smartphones everywhere we go, and

sometimes have a couple of connected devices on us in work, we need to be very wary of being lured into stuff that just doesn't add value to our days. Everybody from Google, Apple, Facebook and Amazon, right through to millions of app developers and content producers, is after our time. Time that we spend with them equals more money in their bank accounts but far more importantly it equals even less time to ourselves and less money in our own bank accounts.

To manage technology properly, you need to be focused and establish what is actually helping you and what is hindering you and eating up your time. I now prefer to have five apps – email, Twitter and a few others – that I use every day and nothing more. They are the apps that help me achieve my goals and what I need to focus on and nothing else.

I have been incredibly lucky to have some wonderful friends around me throughout my life. But while they are essential to provide a sound base – love, support and everything else that we need to survive – the people who love you can very often be the ones who inhibit you the most. The husband who is happy for you to stay at home minding the kids while he jets off achieving his own goals. The parents who are absolutely intent on you going to college and leading a 'respectable' life and gently pouring scorn on your ambitions to become a professional musician. I've always found my loved ones incredibly supportive – but it's usually after the fact, especially when

I have told them the apparently ludicrous things I am thinking of doing in advance! The reality is that people who want the best for you can hold you back from achieving your dreams.

It may sound a bit harsh, but to get shit done you are probably going to have to break free from loved ones and chart your own course. Your parents are probably not going to be over the moon when you walk in and say you are not attending college but going to learn how to be a sky-diving instructor in Canada. They can see only the danger and that fact that you'll be in a faraway place, and it also doesn't fit into the vision they had for you. So you must learn to be honest with people and continue to pursue your own personal goals wherever possible. Just because your parents have put you through school, paid your college fees and supported you for a quarter of a century doesn't mean that you should take a clerical job in a law firm if playing the piano is the one thing that you have always been passionate about.

Of course, this is more challenging when you are part of a couple and have children. You suddenly have people who are dependent on you and you start making the decisions that are no longer just right for you as a person but right for the collective. There is absolutely nothing wrong with that and it is admirable to put the needs of others first when they clearly love you and, in the case of children, depend on you. But just because you have children you shouldn't abandon your dreams. You and your partner need to sit down and work out the goals that are important to each of you individually and how to pursue them while still meeting your responsibilities as parents.

Nobody is going to want exactly the same things from life as you do. The chances of your dreams being aligned with somebody else's are tiny, so to get shit done you may sometimes have to break out from your group of loved ones and go it alone. It isn't easy at first, doing the polar opposite of what your nearest and dearest want you to do, but I'm sure many transatlantic sailors or Hollywood actors had parents who worried about them and cautioned them not to follow such a foolish path. If you want to get shit done you sometimes need to go with your own instincts and ignore what everybody else is saying.

8

Get ahead – go mobile

I'm sure this is one of the first book chapters to be written entirely on a mobile device. I wrote every word on my smartphone. Mobile is taking over the world, and I wanted to understand properly this phenomenon that is so important as to be changing human behaviour across the globe. I wanted to know both the possibilities and also the limitations of mobile. To truly understand a medium you have to immerse yourself in it. What are the hacks to get stuff done quicker? What are the drawbacks? The opportunities?

I've never seen anything be so widely adopted and change so many lives as the smartphone. To understand the wonder of this technology, have a look at a two-year-old swiping one to fire up cartoons or an elderly man using an iPad as if he had owned one all his life. It is a revolution, and possibly the biggest thing to happen in tech in generations. Take the Hailo taxi app, which is available in cities around the world. Here is an app that has transformed an industry for the better in a matter of months. I'm not surprised that consumers have embraced it, but to see ageing cabbies pulling up their apps and increasing their productivity via a smartphone blew my mind. Give people a tool that makes them more money and you'll be surprised at just how quickly they'll adopt it. This sort of disruption is happening across all sorts of industries and it is happening because of the supercomputers (otherwise known as phones) that nearly all of us carry around in our pockets.

In some ways this was the easiest chapter to write. My phone is rarely out of reach whereas I don't always have my laptop with me. I wrote parts of it on the toilet. On buses. In the pub watching football matches and in restaurants while my dining companion popped out to the bathroom. I didn't miss any ideas I had for this chapter because as soon as something came into my head I just whipped out the phone and tapped it in. When I told people I was writing an entire chapter on my phone their initial reaction was that I must be mad, but it was an incredibly exciting and liberating experience. Getting shit done is a way of thinking and a way of living, and nothing epitomizes it better than working on your phone when you would otherwise be simply killing time. Just because we have never used a phone as a word processor before doesn't mean it can't be done.

While many laud social media as the defining technology of our era, I'd argue that it is going mobile that has changed the game completely, and in particular the unveiling of the iPhone in 2007. We take it for granted now that we all have an online computer, phone, media player, hard drive, picture taker and video maker all in one tiny slim device. Add in apps and that expands to maps, your bank account, radio, TV, streaming media and anything else that you could ever think of. We have more information at our fingertips than most governments or large corporations could access in a month just a couple of decades ago.

Mobile technology has also drastically changed the way many of us work. The nine-to-five work day is something of the past. Employers now expect their employees to be contactable pretty much at any time or place. Most people roll over in the morning and before brushing their teeth grab their phone and check their emails. This has shifted the work–life balance to one that is essentially work–work. To compensate, employers are now often more understanding about people taking time off: you can't refuse somebody an hour for a doctor's appointment when they sit in front of their TV answering emails for you most evenings. As I mentioned in the life hacks chapter, this new mobile way of working provides other opportunities to improve your quality of life by working remotely. We are still at the start of the mobile revolution and by joining it you can stay ahead of everyone else.

For the first time ever, graduates leaving college are more skilled in the most important part of business life than their elders. I've spent a lot of time with executives and older people running businesses and the most common response they have to technology is fear. Change always breeds fear and the pace of change at the moment is truly breathtaking. Software is eating up the world with everything from books and newspapers to retail and finance moving online. Very soon doing stuff online will not be the exception but the norm in nearly every field. So how do you stay on the pace and get in on the action and avoid getting left behind? The answer, unexpectedly, comes from technology itself and it is all about self-tuition.

The traditional, classroom-based way of absorbing knowledge and improving skills was to study books whose contents were explained by teachers. It worked brilliantly for generations and there is still a place for this type of learning. But we now have the internet. This opens up endless possibilities, especially of improving skills. YouTube is a great place to start. There are millions of free videos from the smartest people in the world trying to teach you stuff. You don't have to pay for an MBA in Stanford when most of the lecturers are already sharing their wisdom online. Don't understand how Facebook's targeted advertising really works? Within a few seconds you can be watching a couple of hundred detailed tutorials about it from some of the world's best marketers. Want to learn how to brew your own beer and start a microbrewery in your spare time? Forget about going to classes and just research it all on your phone on the train into work.

However, the one thing that I would most strongly encourage you to learn online is a small amount of computer coding. Now you probably think this has nothing to do with the line of work you are in. You don't have to know how to write your own website from scratch or build an app, but you should appreciate that code is starting to take over the world and if possible find out a bit about it. Everything from our cars, fridges, newspapers and homes are starting to be powered by computer code.

Ones and zeros. See, the majority of us live in complete ignorance about the most important thing happening in the world today, so learning a small bit of code will give you an advantage over 99 per cent of the population.

Over a weekend seven years ago I learned basic HTML (it stands for Hypertext Markup Language) when my friends were away and I had nothing to do. It is the single most important piece of learning I have ever completed in my life. It has allowed me to launch blogs, talk to developers in their own language about websites and informed my thinking on everything from phone selection to my privacy settings. I don't know how to build anything substantial but I understand the very basic building blocks of the internet and technology from those three days spent learning online. The beauty here is that there are a bunch of online tools that will help you learn to code. You can take a few lessons in places like Code Academy at your own pace and build up your knowledge as you go. Even if you think it is too late for yourself and you have no interest you might have children or siblings who could benefit from learning to code. The wonderful Irish-led initiative CoderDojo offers free coding clubs for young people, allowing them to learn these skills through communal classes. Indeed, today it is probably more beneficial for children to be learning computer code than a second or third language. Coding is the new Latin.

I despair when I hear people, young or old, say that technology is passing them by and that they don't know where to start. I worked in marketing for four years and even though that entire industry was moving online, because that is where consumers are spending their time these days, people in it were still pleading ignorance. I also saw that the handful of smart and resourceful people who were willing to throw themselves into the new world and teach themselves were able to make huge strides in their careers and progress far faster than they ever could have otherwise.

For the first internet generation, trying to set up a business was both a serious challenge and a costly exercise. Accountants would need to be hired, websites built from scratch, software licences bought, expensive marketing campaigns devised to attract customers and market research carried out in the real world. A typical tech start-up during the dot-com era, for example, would have needed hundreds of thousands if not millions in investment to build the tech infrastructure they needed. Luckily, we now live in an age where you can get a start-up business up and running for less than a few hundred dollars anywhere in the world. You can do it sitting on a beach in Tahiti or in a basement in Moscow and with those few hundred dollars, a good idea and some super execution you can go on to change the world. While many entrepreneurs try to raise capital from outside investors before starting the business, the reality is that it is usually far better to use your own limited funds to grow your company (also known as bootstrapping) and to take advantage of free online tools to build as much value into it as possible before you start offering shares in it to other people. That way, when the profits start to roll in you get to keep them all rather than handing over a chunk of cash to your investors. Of course, that doesn't apply to every business because for some you will still need significant capital investment for some physical or intellectual property related businesses, but when it comes to the online world or software the barriers to entry couldn't be lower. The bottom line is that you could start a good business today with a laptop, an internet connection and a credit card.

So what tools have I used over the years that you should know about and how can they be used to take advantage of this new world? Here are just five that I wouldn't be able to live without.

Google Apps

We run the entire admin side of our business using Google Apps. For €50 a year you get unlimited email, online calendars, documents, spreadsheets, presentations and everything else you need to run a business. It is essentially an online version of Microsoft Office without the prohibitive licensing fees and it all lives in the Cloud. You can have it up and running in five minutes and add or remove users as you need them. The collaboration tools such as chat within email, mobile versions of the site and ease of use mean that the entire back-end of your office is set up in minutes. I really don't know what I'd do without it.

Amazon Hosting

Hosting websites, apps and services that are going to scale or grow in size used to be a massive pain in the ass and an expensive business. Not many people know about AWS (Amazon Web Services) outside the techie world. It is essentially Cloud hosting and it has allowed companies like Pinterest, Airbnb and Foursquare to scale as quickly as they have without having to constantly worry about servers. You pay according to the amount of bandwidth you use and can keep close control of costs without suffering the crippling overheads usually associated with ramping up a business.

Skype

You perhaps associate Skype with chatting to your grandparents on the other side of the world or catching up with family or friends, but it is just as useful in a business context. Why pay for an office switchboard, international phone calls and conferencing software when you can get it all for free? Some of the most innovative and exciting start-ups I see use Skype; it literally allows you to spread employees and contractors out all over the world and keep in touch with them for free while sitting in your boxer shorts in your living room.

LinkedIn

Personal social networks such as Twitter and Facebook are great for content, interaction and to keep up with our friends, but from a business perspective there has never been a tool quite like LinkedIn. Anybody can set up a free profile and after building a small network you will be able to contact all sorts of people who could be of interest. Everybody from CEOs to founders of start-ups right through to HR and purchasing managers maintain a professional presence on the site. Starting a company today or looking for a job has never been easier as you can tap into the entire demographic of the business world.

Basecamp

There are hundreds of project management tools out there but I've been using Basecamp for the last five years and found no more effective way to get an overview of my business or to manage a large amount of staff and projects through one central resource. I can log in at any time from anywhere and get an instant snapshot of my organization, find files that we have been working on as well as keep track of the work people have done. In terms of running a company it is absolutely vital. They offer a free trial and there is then a small monthly subscription which is well worth paying.

The big advantage you have as a small business or a start-up is that you can choose the tools you use. The internet, mobile and the Cloud have given us a range of options that our predecessors never had and we should count ourselves very lucky. As a start-up you will be up against larger businesses who have big overheads and complicated legacy systems but these five cheap or free tools along with your choice of the hundreds of others out there will give you a massive advantage in terms of getting shit done for free and building something remarkable at very little cost.

In the early days of Simply Zesty Lauren and I realized that we weren't good at dealing with people. We could handle staff, customers and suppliers but going out there and networking was a serious pain and something we just didn't enjoy. Some people are just born networkers and can walk into a room, make friends with pure strangers and win business in an instant. I'm not one of them. I'm good when I know people well but with strangers I tend to look at my feet muttering inanities to the point that people think I'm a weirdo. On the rare occasions that I do find myself at networking events I'm the guy getting coffee and looking at the biscuits as if my life depended on it, hoping somebody will strike up a conversation with me instead of me having to approach them. So, without a network and seriously shy, I decided to find another way to go about it and that was to network online.

There are four main social networks: Twitter, Facebook, LinkedIn and YouTube. You can also set up your own blog. I'd suggest that you find the two that you are most comfortable with and really focus on them. LinkedIn might seem like the obvious choice for business and it has super potential for gaining leads but I use it only to find contacts within companies rather than to network. I've always maintained a presence on LinkedIn and Facebook but have never invested the time or energy needed to create meaningful connections. It is tempting to try to take on all five, and many do, but I'd argue that you are far better off concentrating on two and doing them really well. The two I have always focused on are Twitter and blogging because I love creating content for those platforms and I interact well with people there.

Online networking allows me to focus on making connections with the people I want to rather than walking into a room where at least 80 per cent of those in it are of no use to me. When you network in the real world you waste lots of time trying to find that one good connection: the proverbial needle in a haystack. If you work at it hard enough, over time you will build an online network that is far more powerful than anything in the real world and you can choose to meet only the people who are useful to you.

Of course, you can only take an online relationship so

far, and a personal meeting will go a long way towards taking the relationship to the next level. So although it is a brilliant way to interact with people you might otherwise never encounter, don't forget that at the end of the day we are all human. Online tools are a wonderful way to bypass all the nonsense that is involved in the early days of networking but once you do make a connection be sure to transfer that relationship into a real and meaningful personal one as well.

Twitter is the most remarkable tool I have come across in terms of networking. I can guarantee that pretty much everybody in your industry you'll ever want to connect with is on there. Journalists use it heavily. Investors all have a presence. It is like gaining instant access to everyone you ever wanted to meet and you can do it while sitting in your pyjamas with a beer watching the match.

I've been able to win a couple of million euros' worth of business as a direct result of Twitter. The best example was a European marketing manager for a large brand who tweeted looking for a local agency in Ireland to execute a campaign for them. At the time in Simply Zesty we had only three employees and were just about bursting out of my spare room so we were in no way ready for the work. Nobody in Ireland had spotted the tweet but a guy in my own network with just seventeen followers did. Turns out I'd been talking to him the night before about social media and had answered a question of his about Facebook. I'd solved a problem for him. When he saw the brand manager tweeting he immediately suggested Simply Zesty and introduced the brand manager to me. After a quick chat, a couple of phone calls and a pitch over the phone in which I played up our credentials as one of the biggest agencies in Ireland we were awarded a €30,000 contract. We went on to win €100,000 of work from that client and form a meaningful relationship that lasts until this day.

None of that would have happened without the guy with seventeen followers. He was the key to all this and the story explains why you should care more about the quality of your interactions than your follow count. Recall my notion of planting 10,000 seeds from Chapter 3. Sure, 99 per cent of those seeds aren't going to sprout, and you'll help loads of people and get nothing in return, but if you keep sowing those seeds and engaging with people those that do grow will reward you a hundred times over. I've found talented staff, people to renovate my house, new cars, investors, customers and even dates on Twitter. The key is being unselfish. The mistake a lot of people make is to start tweeting about how amazing they are. You wouldn't walk into a networking event or a pub and shout 'Look at me!' and neither should you on Twitter. Instead, share wonderful information, help people and forget about the followers and you'll be stunned by the results you get.

There are a number of ways in which you can help people and the first is through the content that you share. Linking to your own website or business isn't the best idea because people can smell self-promotion a mile off. No harm in doing it once in a while, but the best way to get followers and meaningful interaction is to share great information. You also have to share information that will build you into an expert in your own area. It doesn't matter if you are a Danish pig farmer or a UK politician running for election, you need to share the best links, the best photos, the stuff that will make people click on the follow button and make them feel like they never want to miss an update from you ever again. People follow me because they know they'll get articles about marketing or social media that they'll never see anywhere else. You can absolutely do the same, and even if you have only a handful of followers you need to start sharing that information right now. I'm not going to lie and say that it happens overnight or that there is some sort of magic viral button that you can push because it just doesn't work like that, but I guarantee the results will come with time.

Most people have a day job or stuff that keeps them away from Twitter, so how do you find time to tweet fifty times a day? To interact with others and share the best information? Well, I build it into my day. The mobile is key and I'll whip it out – in queues, on planes, in the toilet, when shopping, in the pub or in the back of a taxi – and simply interact with people. Sure, what else are you going to be doing anyway? You can even incorporate it into the work day by doing larger pieces of work (say forty-five minutes to an hour) and then spending five minutes tweeting a few brilliant links or interacting with others. Another trick is to schedule tweets (HootSuite, TweetDeck and other services allow you to do this) the night before. So in the evening while watching TV find half a dozen links, photos or articles that you want to share the following day and simply queue them up. By using a mixture of these tricks you can give the illusion that you are 'always on' while enjoying a relatively stress-free time.

I have seen people distracted by social media, Twitter in particular, to the point where it interferes with them getting shit done. Refreshing the feed looking for new content can be like an addictive drug. The key is to see it as a means to an end. Sure, it is entertaining, but what are you trying to get out of it? What are the core metrics that you are using it for? Is it for new business? To drive traffic to a website? To build your brand? Always have that in mind and measure the benefits over time to see if Twitter is the right channel for you. It certainly is for me but with social networking there are many ways to skin a cat. Patience and commitment are key.

Social networks come and go. Myspace and Bebo were pre-eminent at one time. Twitter and Facebook dominate today and new networks and utilities will emerge in the future. When people try to build their brand they often focus on getting likes, followers or fans on the site of the day. I did it way back in 2006 when Digg was a powerful driver of traffic and referrals and I spent hundreds of hours trying to become a 'super user'. Digg quickly died off and my hours of work were rendered useless. I've nothing to show for them today. Although such trends come and go, one thing I can confidently predict will never vanish is your own blog. Blogging is the most powerful tool I know when it comes to building your own brand or that of your company. It is your own corner of the web that you will always own, that will never go out of fashion and which you control every aspect of.

The biggest problem I find is that blogging has a certain stigma attached to it from the early days when the blogosphere was a bit of an unregulated Wild West and people could and did say pretty much whatever they wanted. There's also a perception that you need some vast tech knowledge to get one started. Once you understand that a blog is essentially a personal website that you can set up in next to no time using free software and that posting on it is easier than sending an email you'll quickly see the benefits.

There are only two platforms worth considering and both are free. Blogger is owned by Google and you can have a blog set up in minutes, but I'd strongly suggest you use WordPress. There are hundreds of free templates that you can use and you could be posting content almost immediately.

Another preconception is that you have to write 2,000 words of lofty prose at a time. You could easily share pictures, videos or audio instead. You might post pictures of the flowers in the garden, shoes celebrities are wearing or your thoughts on African chimpanzees. Your blog's content is limited only by your imagination. The technology and platforms are so easy to use these days that embedding a video or uploading a photo is no harder than anything you would do on Facebook, so playing the tech Luddite card is no longer possible.

The beauty of a blog is that, unlike traditional media such as newspapers or magazines, you don't have to have a PR strategy or go around begging for coverage because you are producing the content yourself. You are the journalist. The artist. The film-maker. You are whatever you want to be. In most cases writing about yourself or your business isn't going to be very exciting and you won't get many readers. People couldn't give two shits about the awards your business won or your latest hires. That information is only of interest to you. What you need to do is create compelling content that people will be looking for online. So on my blog I share tips for entrepreneurs. Things I did to help start my own business. Failures I've had. Lists of tools to get you started. None of those are going to help me but they are designed to keep readers coming back for more. Nothing is as powerful as sharing your knowledge. People bookmark those posts. Share them with their friends. Lecturers use them.

When we set up Simply Zesty we didn't have a marketing budget. We didn't have deep contacts with decision makers within the industry. We were small fry and would get small-budget work as a result. We decided we needed an entirely new approach so we started a blog. While most agencies hide their 'ideas' and are in effect selling their special sauce and creativity we decided to give every ounce of knowledge we had away. Social media was new, with brands and other agencies struggling to make heads or tails of it, so we did it for them. Because the information was useful to others over 500,000 people per month were coming to the blog at its height. You could argue that 99 per cent of them were taking the ideas and using them for their own clients but we were able to make a business out of the 1 per cent who saw us as experts and hired us.

Blogging isn't easy and it requires a lot of initial effort for very little return, but if you want to set yourself up as an expert in a particular field in this day and age there is no better way to get shit done and get your name out there.

Let's face it, we are in business to make money and if you are going to be a success then you need customers. Travel back a couple of decades and customers were typically found by getting out there and shaking hands, delivering great service to attract repeat business or through expensive marketing campaigns. We live in a very different world today where people find most of their goods and services online. If you want a new vacuum cleaner you'll search for some reviews. Need insurance for your car and you'll likely visit a comparison website. Rather than pulling out the phone book to find a plumber or a solicitor you'll ask friends on Twitter or trawl through Google. The choice for consumers has never been greater, and for that we should be very grateful, but when it comes to getting customers for your own business the game has changed dramatically. There are a number of tools I use for my own businesses, for start-ups I advise or in my own personal life and I never cease to be amazed either by just how effective they are in terms of getting shit done or by how few businesses are actually aware of them. Here are five of my favourite tools for attracting customers.

Google Ads

Google is one of the most valuable companies in the world for one main reason: their targeted advertising. When people go to search for products or services today they do so primarily via Google. For a small fee you can insert your adverts above those search results so that consumers are likely to visit your website first. It is the most targeted advertising ever seen and it is hugely valuable in terms of attracting new customers. You would be a fool not to use it.

Facebook Ads

If Google is the place where people explicitly search for stuff then Facebook is the place where they spend time browsing. It is the newspaper for the modern generation and the amount of data they can collect about us all to help advertisers is remarkable. If you are trying to target males between twenty and thirty who live in England and who like Coldplay then you need to be advertising on

Facebook. No matter how niche your product or how random the audience you want to attract, Facebook has the targeting ability to reach those people for a very low cost.

Content Marketing

In the old days the media used to create most of the content that we consumed and brands would pay for adverts around that content. Now that consumers are becoming a lot more savvy at ignoring ads, brands are creating their own content. As a business or brand you need to be creating your own content to attract customers. It might be 'how to' guides, instructional videos or pretty infographics, but whatever it is you need to be doing it. Consumers are spending more and more of their time on social media these days so if you can create content that reaches them and draws them into your website, app or services they will become your customers.

Retargeting

No other form of advertising is more effective at attracting new customers or making you seem much bigger than you actually are. A potential customer only has to visit your website once and from that moment on via cookies (an internet tracking tool) they'll be shown your ads wherever they go. It is very cheap for an advertiser but whether the consumer goes to the BBC, the *New York Times* or CNN they'll be seeing your ads on those sites. A massively useful tool to help attract customers.

Email Marketing

Using email to attract customers is nothing new, but it is the technology that just keeps on giving. When you think about it the first thing most of us do in the morning or when we arrive in work is to check our emails. We might not be on any of the social networks but we all need email to get our work done. If you can come up with creative ways to get people to sign up to your emails and then keep them engaged with smart content you will get more customers than you could ever imagine.

It doesn't matter just how niche your product is because by using today's technology and some smart thinking you can be attracting the first customers to your product or service within a couple of hours of launch. The long tail of the internet means that there are always people looking for what you are trying to sell and the tools to connect with those customers are there for you to use.

An excellent example of all of this in action today is PR Slides, my current company. We are essentially a platform that provides images for the media to use free of charge. Companies pay to have their images on the site and the benefit is that the media use their images and they get free PR. We are the middle men who need to get the brands there but far more important is that we attract journalists to the site. Journalists are bombarded with advertising and they are hard people to connect with so we use very precise online marketing to make sure that we target the needle-in-a-haystack problem using the following three-stage process:

1 Attract journalists to the site through content marketing

We create lots of different content to drag journalists into the site. We hold online awards for the best journalist in a specific country to get their attention. We also target them with ads based on their profession on LinkedIn, Facebook, Twitter and Google, which are the services that they use every day to do their job. If a journalist logs on the chances are they are going to be drawn into our site through one of our content marketing strategies and it doesn't cost us a lot of money.

2 Retarget them with constant ads

All visitors to our site are subsequently tracked by cookies and therefore are open to retargeting. This means that rather than spraying banner ads around the internet hoping that a journalist will see them we can follow their every move with an advert. Most sites are signed up to the Google network so even when journalists are browsing their personal interests like sports, culture or eating out they will still be seeing our ads. This is not only a great way to build brand awareness for a small start-up but also means that, since they have visited the site once, they are far more likely to click on the ad and sign up for our product.

3 Reel them in with email marketing

Once a journalist has signed up to our service we want to make sure that we stay front-of-mind at all times. They'll have entered their email address so we make sure to follow up with highly relevant targeted emails that match their interests. You don't want to be spamming them, and the content has to be outstanding, but as soon as you have them hooked at this stage you have a customer for life.

This sort of marketing takes the mystique out of getting new customers and makes it more of an exact science. In the old days you would have needed people on the ground shaking hands and getting to know hundreds of journalists, which would have cost a fortune in time and money. Of course, you still must have an amazing product that people actually want to use, but getting new customers, and as a result getting shit done, has never been easier or more scientific than it is today.

You might think that cash is king and that the debit and credit cards in your wallet are always going to be the future of commerce. That's understandable: we've had a really good relationship with physical goods as far back as the Romans or the Vikings, at first bartering and later attaching a monetary value to them. But that is all changing in front of our eyes as we move towards a truly digital currency. On an average month for the last decade €3–4,000 has gone in and out of my personal bank account to cover my various day-to-day expenditures. In the last six months, though, I've seen an unprecedented change in that as everything moves towards my mobile device and digital currency. I can see a day coming in the next three or four years when I will use nothing but my phone as my wallet and we need to be very aware of this transition at both a personal and a business level. If I look at the last month alone I have gambled money online using my smartphone, I've booked flights, paid for accommodation on Airbnb, paid for taxis and even bought concert tickets on it. I've been watching TV, seen something I like, pulled out my phone and bought that product there and then. I've gone from spending none of my disposable income online (I was never a big online shopper) to doing over 50 per cent of my transactions there. Even if I owe somebody money now for a couple of beers I'll take out my phone and send it to them with a couple of clicks.

It is one thing for us to consume media or engage with our friends via mobile devices, but when we start spending money on our phones and trading using a purely digital currency the world needs to sit up and pay attention. Bitcoin, Stripe and in-app purchases are showing that not only is there an appetite for a digital economy but that it is the way our entire society is heading. It might seem like a big scary world that you have little or no influence on personally but if I was a bricks-and-mortar retailer, a politician or a stockbroker these are trends I would like to know about. You can't simply cover your eyes and hope for the best when disruption like this comes along.

The fate of the iconic Kodak company is emblematic of what is happening. Kodak pioneered photography over decades. It was a solid business with a brand that nearly everyone knew just from the logo. But because Kodak failed to embrace technology it quickly started to decline and with costly overheads, and little or no product innovation, it lurched towards bankruptcy. At the same time four individuals set up a company called Instagram. They cobbled their product together very quickly and launched it to iPhone users only. Although their product wasn't identical to Kodak's they captured the imagination of the world in a similar way, allowing people to take photos from their phone, add filters and share them with the world via social media. It was the new 'Kodak moment'. Instagram grew to over 100 million users and although it had only sixteen staff, no revenue and had been trading for just over 1,000 days it was acquired by Facebook for $1 billion. Instagram continued to grow, its user base passing a quarter of a billion and its world-leader status assured, while Kodak went through the bankruptcy courts.

The fate of these two companies illustrates the fact

that we are facing the biggest era of commercial disruption the world has ever seen. There will be massive winners and huge losers and the winners will be those who are aware of what is happening, have no fear of it and are willing to teach themselves and embrace it. We are only at the very start of the mobile revolution and if you want to get ahead in the next decade you should probably bet the house on mobile. Do what I did and teach yourself everything you possibly can about this new world. It might start with writing a long email on a phone instead of your desktop or buying an iPad. Whatever you do, though, don't stand still.

9

Playing ugly, winning ugly

Having enemies is a useful business strategy. It certainly works for me. At different times enemies drive you on in different ways. In the early days of Simply Zesty there was a well-known blogger and online type who was also setting up his own business and he initially helped us with introductions to a couple of clients. We were small time and no threat to his core business. Very quickly, though, we started to grow, and as we did his attitude changed. He never bothered me with his pointed online attacks, and I'd treat them as a joke, but on two separate occasions he picked first on my cousin Mark, who was working as an intern, and then on Lauren. Both were upset, especially Lauren.

This guy suddenly became Enemy Number One to me. I made a vow that I'd beat him. Not just beat him but trample him so far into the ground that he would be sorry he'd ever heard of us. First, even though he was ten times bigger than us, I put every ounce of energy I had into increasing traffic on my blog to match his. I woke up earlier in the mornings because of his stupid little face. Every negative tweet he sent about us made me cycle home that little bit faster so I could get to my keyboard and do something productive against him.

Eventually our blogs' visitor numbers came level, but I didn't feel any satisfaction. I pushed even harder. We needed to be twice as big, I decided. I put that extra hour in at the office. I missed the sporting events. I cancelled dates with friends. Everything I did for a few months I did to beat that bastard and show him that nobody could make my teammates feel that bad and get away with it. In the end, I'd pushed so hard that our blog had ten times as much traffic as his. I channelled the power of my hatred to make myself work harder. It's hardly a conventional technique, but when the snow was coming down and I had a choice between hitting the snooze button or jumping out of bed to beat this guy I always chose the latter. I'd nearly go as far as to say he was key to our early success, because without that sort of drive I might not have made all the sacrifices that I ended up making. Our client list kept growing, the number of staff we employed doubled and our profits increased to the point where his digs at us had no effect whatsoever.

I would never have had that level of motivation without a competitor to beat, and I battled like an Olympian going for gold. This is one reason why people can still have long and successful careers even if they lack innate talent – they will do just about anything to beat the competition.

The key is to keep on finding bigger enemies. More relevant enemies. Within a year we were out of this guy's league, and I had to start picking harder 'targets'. That big firm who had stolen a client from us. International agencies. Finding somebody who makes your blood boil and tackling them head on while focusing on your own game is one of the keys to success. Would Roy Keane have been the great player he was without a rival like Patrick Vieira? Would Ayrton Senna have become such an icon without Alain Prost to battle against? Competition and enemies drag the best out of you and take your performance to another level that you probably didn't even realize you had in you. Seek out enemies and rise above them and not only beat them but crush them into the ground.

The most successful sports teams, businesses and people know how to win ugly. How to grind out a o–1 result in the middle of January when playing horrendously. How to get that one last-minute sale in a week when nothing else is going for you. How to finish a quarter with break-even results when it would have been so much easier to accept a small loss. Everybody will show up when the going is good and sales and results are coming easily, but what you want are the people and the mentality within yourself to get shit done when you need to win ugly. When you've had nine doors slammed in your face, are you able to go and knock on the tenth with as much gusto and energy as you did the first? Brilliant, well-educated employees who will shine when everything is going their way are ten a penny, but who are the ones who are going to be superstars? The ones who'll roll up their sleeves when the shit really hits the fan and everything is falling down around them?

You won't remember the people who were there celebrating the good times with you, toasting you with champagne, but you will remember the couple of friends or employees who were there to scrape you off the floor. Leaders and the most successful people really shine when the chips are down; when they've gone all-in and the cards are against them. At times of crisis I always pause and look at the people around me. Who are the ones keeping their heads down pretending to look for solutions and who is staring you back in the eye, ready for action?

I've an incredible friend called Caroline who has helped me immensely and who typifies the sort of person everyone should have in their lives. Our paths crossed a couple of years back when she briefly dated my best friend Sean. That fizzled out, but she and I remained in touch. This was a period when I was struggling with the booze big time and more or less self-destructing. I had hit rock bottom, hiding from everybody I knew and going on a seven-day bender. A massive binge. Caroline managed to help me through it and refused to desert me, staying by my side as I drained a bottle of vodka and holding my hand as I battled the shakes and tried to sleep it off so I could go clean again. I begged her to live her own life but she wouldn't; instead, recognizing somebody in need, she made the hard call. Because she was there for me and she cared, I found the strength to end my binge. When I woke up the next morning there she was, waiting for me, showing that she'd help.

Instead of legging it as most people would in that

situation she toughed it out because she saw my drinking as a cry for help and believed there was someone worth saving inside the drunken mess. At that time Caroline was working as a retail salesperson – the ultimate dead-end job – and thoroughly fed up with both her life and her career. I remember thinking to myself that one day I'd repay her and show the same belief in her that she had in me when nobody else had. Two years passed and we grew closer as I found my feet.

Today Caroline is head of sales in PR Slides, with a team of six working for her in one of the most exciting tech start-ups in the world (yes, I would say that, wouldn't I, but the numbers also back it up), and remains one of my closest friends. I trust her completely, having learned everything about her I needed to years ago. She wasn't even thinking about a new job when she helped me, but when things got ugly she was there. I employ her on merit, and because month on month she delivers great sales numbers, but I also have an incredible ally who would walk through a wall for me if I asked her to.

No matter what happens, or how things go personally or professionally, I know that if the shit ever hits the fan again Caroline won't go running. She won't hide or blame others or sugar-coat facts for me because in my darkest moments I saw what she was willing to do for somebody she barely knew. It takes a long time to find the people you need to surround yourself with, but you are going to have a lot of battles and a lot of lows and it's vital to have friends and colleagues who are willing to fight alongside you and who won't run off at the first sign of trouble. When I sat slurring my words in a daze, believing I might die, I didn't ever think that Caroline would be a key business partner and somebody I'd rely on to help me grow, but that's exactly what she is.

Should you lie to get shit done? You'll be surprised to hear that the answer is yes. You have to do right by people, not screw them around or generally be reckless, but you'll find that telling a few untruths is, on the odd occasion, not only useful but downright essential. Before you go jumping on your moral high horse, let me give you an example. When we are chasing sales I sometimes set an unrealistically high target. If I want to achieve €50,000 in revenue for the month I'll keep that figure to myself and tell the team working for me we are chasing €100,000. Not only that, but I'll also tell them that the business could fold if we don't get that number, and that our investors will go ballistic. As the month goes on, I'll say that we are miles behind and that we'll have to work every hour under the sun and kill ourselves to get there.

What usually happens is that we end up at €75–80,000, which is short of the fake target but massively above the business plan. Human nature is to do the minimum necessary to reach our goals, so if I'd asked for €50,000, that's probably all I'd have got. By lying, you can tap the full potential of your sales force. With a higher target a new sense of focus is there from day one and people double down on effort. Sometimes against all expectations you'll even get the €100,000, which is double what you have in the business plan and a good place to be.

So what are the downsides to lying? First and foremost, it is morally suspect, so you have to get comfortable with that concept. I try to make amends by ensuring staff always get their bonuses on time and giving them a little more than they expected. (You might have to tell another white lie that you have saved costs elsewhere to balance the books and that it isn't all doom and gloom despite 'missing' the target.) Everyone perks up when they receive a bigger-than-anticipated bonus, and you can give them a big night out and a pat on the back to show how much you appreciate their effort.

You clearly can't do this too often because people will soon catch on, but if you are feeling under pressure it's a way of getting your staff to share the load and get even bigger shit done. It is another example of winning ugly, but it will help you achieve bigger and better things. You don't want to become a habitual liar because that isn't going to get you very far in the long run, but the odd white lie can be very beneficial.

Similarly, there are times when you have to bullshit, pretend to be something you're not. I wouldn't call it lying, but you do have to be flexible with the truth. I remember the early days of Simply Zesty when it was just Lauren and me in my spare bedroom. Taxis were out of the question because we needed every penny we had to keep the wolf away from the door. We used to drive everywhere on a battered old Vespa because it only cost us about €3 a week to run and it got us to meetings quicker than any other mode of transport. There wasn't a week that winter when one of us wasn't ill from the freezing cold, skidding through the Dublin ice.

One of our biggest clients in the early days was Vodafone. Because social media was so new and we were pretty much the only gig in town they appointed us to oversee a couple of small campaigns. We'd drive up to their office on the scooter and park a good bit down the road before walking into the foyer as if we owned the place. Although I rarely dress to impress I'd taken to wearing suit jackets and slacks with smart shoes and Lauren was also suitably well attired. We'd walk into meetings and talk about 'the team back in the office' and our 'video department' and say 'we'll have to check that with our accounts director'. Little did Vodafone or any other of our large clients know that our entire operation had arrived on the back of that Vespa, freezing their asses off without a penny between them.

This was all going well until Vodafone said they were so happy with our work that they wanted to appoint us as their full-time social media agency. This would mean vetting us to make sure we were what we said we were, which we definitely were not. We managed to blag our way through it until they asked if the next meeting could be in our offices. 'Fuck,' we both said as we walked out the door, 'we've just lost the account.' This was a disaster. The client responsible for 70 per cent of our revenue and without whom we couldn't pay the bills was surely about to pull the plug. We'd successfully convinced them of the Emperor's new clothes, but if the tide washed out we'd be caught wearing no clothes whatsoever.

After a few emergency meetings in my back room we quickly decided there was no alternative but to keep bluffing in the hope we'd somehow get away with it. Citing an 'impossible workload' and the ferocious growth we were going through, we postponed for a month. When the month passed there were illnesses and more important meetings to attend. Eventually, the site visit was forgotten and we were appointed Vodafone's main social media agency with a big retainer. We quickly managed to hire staff and snagged such nice offices that we were only too happy to welcome them, but it was a very close shave.

Too many people hold their hands up and tell the truth in business when it is better to bluff. We didn't outright lie, although we certainly created a false impression. But we were young, hungry and doing the best work of all their agencies for a much smaller fee, so surely some bullshit was justified. Sometimes the rules are there to be bent, and even if you are winning ugly and hanging on by the skin of your teeth you do what you have to. Somebody asked me at a conference whether bullshit was ethical and I couldn't answer. The only thing I could say was that if we hadn't made those calls and taken those chances we'd more than likely have gone out of business. Faced with that stark reality, I didn't mind lashing on a suit and striding into hotels all over the capital to meet clients because we were 'too busy to meet back in our own offices'. Needs must.

Winning ugly is doing the things that nobody else wants to do, not just once but over and over again. The term winning ugly is heard often in sport and is something most teams (or, indeed, individuals) need to do at some point if they are to finish first, no matter what the discipline. A football team, for example, typically plays forty or so league games over a season, and it is the sides that win even when they don't deserve to that end up at the top of the pile. The best teams are more than the sum of their individual members, be it in a sporting sense or a business sense, and you all have to be in it together. Sure, the greatest teams in the world are packed full of stars with outrageous talent, but they also epitomize what winning ugly is all about. Although you'll see incredible moves and sublime skill, the one thing that sets them apart is hard work. The chasing down of apparently lost causes when it would be easier to put their hands on their hips. The covering of every blade of grass on the pitch even when they have a handsome lead.

Getting shit done means doing everything you possibly can to achieve your goals, be it as an individual or as a team, and sometimes that means winning ugly. When the rain is smashing into my face on a cold dark morning going into work I take pride in walking faster and having a bigger smile on my face. I know that most people are letting the elements, tiredness and what they think of as bad luck get them down. I know that on a bad day I can pull further away from the competition than I can on a good one. Lifting the mood of staff on bad days and refilling them with confidence will have a much bigger impact than a pat on the back when things have gone well. If you can encourage yourself or your team to win ugly when things are going against you then you will get all sorts of crazy shit done.

When I was a child, my family lived in Belgium. I was flying over to Ireland via Manchester with my dad for my grandfather's funeral and as we neared the airport on a cold stormy night close to midnight most people were nodding off as we made our final approach. A couple of hundred feet off the ground there was a serious jolt and the engines screamed and we were off up into the air again. People gasped and the captain came on to say that there had been a 'minor issue' but not to worry because we would be landing shortly. You could suddenly cut the tension in the plane with a knife. Everybody was alert and looking round for signs of what might be happening.

As we came in the second time the same thing happened. This time the captain told us that the flaps had frozen over and that he would be making another attempt to 'jam them out' before trying to land again. Now people were holding each other and praying. We eventually landed on the fourth attempt and the passengers broke out into spontaneous applause. That night the airline put us all up in a hotel and I've never seen a group of people drink so much. There was a feeling of joy at surviving such a close shave. My whole perception of flying changed that night. Until then I'd flown many times and never been even slightly worried, but I'd just seen how close to the edge you can come when in a large piece of metal at 37,000 feet doing 700 mph.

I had to fly back to Brussels on my own as Dad was staying on and I was due back at school. I was already super nervous when the air hostess sat me down in the front row and we headed off. I could feel myself twitching and more alert than usual. I had to transfer in London and the weather was incredibly stormy as we approached Heathrow. As we rocked from side to side through the storm the plane suddenly shook violently as a bright flash lit up the sky. Electric blue streaks sparked along the wings and I realized we had been hit by lightning. Once again the captain reassured us, saying that planes regularly suffer lightning strikes and that this was all very routine. I don't really remember landing but I do remember being first off the plane and hearing a member of the ground crew saying to the stewardess, 'I hear you took a direct hit up there,' to which she replied, 'Yeah, very close call.'

From that moment onwards I was terrified of flying. I'd one more short hop to take from London to Brussels and I remember thinking I simply couldn't get on that flight, the state I was in. I had two hours and, although I was only fourteen, went straight to the duty-free shop and bought eight cans of Guinness on the pretext that they were for my parents. I then sat in the toilets and downed six of them and walked on to the next plane sideways with the giggles and not a care in the world. Desperate times called for desperate measures and even at that young age I knew that booze had near magical powers.

After that I avoided flying whenever possible. When I did have to fly I got so nervous that I would count the seconds of every minute we were in the air. I'd have stupid little superstitions like touching the ground before I got on the plane (because it might be the last time I'd ever touch it, I told myself). I even started praying and promising to do wonderful things if God just got me through the flight. I'd nearly have a nervous breakdown every time the pitch of the engine changed. I'd grab the arm rests as if my life depended on it and I would insist on a certain seat number, checking in three hours early to make sure I got it. I'd never fly on a Friday and I was absolutely terrified that thirteen minutes past the hour of every flight was the moment the plane would go down. In short I was a babbling mess and I'd start worrying about a flight at least a month in advance.

This stupid behaviour went on for ten years and it really started to mess with my life, from missed job opportunities to abandoned travel plans even through to missing important events like friends' weddings and birthdays because I was so scared of flying. Of course, as a bulletproof male in my early twenties I didn't want to admit any of that and I either concocted excuses or just got so drunk and messy that I barely remembered the flights.

In the end it was the scariest possible situation that got me over it all. I was working on yachts in the Caribbean and needed to fly between ships. When I turned up at the airport my ticket actually said 'Co-Pilot', which I presumed was some sort of joke. It turned out that it was a tiny plane that held only six people and I was indeed sitting beside the captain. I pretty much shat myself on the spot. As we banked between clouds and the plane rattled all around me I suddenly forgot about all the fear. This was the scariest situation I was ever going to be in but the captain showed me some little things in the cockpit and how easy it was to control a plane. Something just clicked in my brain that day and all fear was gone.

When I was just twenty-one I was handed my first head chef's job. I was pretty good at cooking, but I didn't have a clue about management. I had seven staff in the kitchen and I was by far the youngest. My first job was to sack somebody who was no longer needed. Sacking a family man with a couple of kids who depended on his salary was quite an introduction to the realities of being a boss. I really struggled with management in those early days and I started to make the mistake that a lot of managers make: being friends with the staff. I'd take the guys for pints after work, encourage them to share their problems with me and tell them not to worry too much when they made mistakes. We were all in this together and all that.

It seemed to be working great for a couple of weeks as everybody rowed in behind me, but I could feel things slipping. Instead of people being terrified when they made mistakes they'd laugh and say, 'Ah sorry, Niall. Sure, it'll be grand.' The food started suffering. There was no going back. I'd fudged the boundaries between my role and theirs and I'd lost control. Things got worse over the next couple of weeks to the point where everybody had started slacking off, coming in late and dropping their standards. This was my first big management problem and I had no idea how to resolve it. I inevitably turned to booze and let off some steam with them over that night's pints.

As I walked in at midday the next day, hoping that my 'mates' would have gotten on top of things, a scene of chaos greeted me. The fish delivery that had been there since 9 a.m. still hadn't been put away. There was a huge pile of dirty washing. I went out the back to find five of the staff sitting down to a full cooked breakfast, smoking cigarettes. They barely acknowledged my arrival. I realized that being friends with people clearly hadn't worked and that I had completely lost control. I felt an anger bubbling up that I'd never experienced before. I called the lads out to the kitchen to ask them what was going on. As they traipsed out laughing I started explaining about the fish. I got a couple of bullshit excuses and I could feel myself getting angrier. Before I knew it I'd picked up a stack of twenty plates that had just been polished and thrown them on the floor with all my might. I called them a bunch of lazy bastards who had completely disrespected me.

People jumped straight to work. I've never seen a mess be cleaned up as quickly and the fish was in the fridge before I knew it. For the rest of that day the kitchen ran with military precision as people tiptoed around me and worked flawlessly. I won't lie and say everything was perfect after that but I learned a massive lesson that day in terms of making people respect you. There are better ways to do it rather than losing the rag and throwing plates, but without a healthy dose of fear, respect and control you will never get the best out of people. You just can't be proper friends with everybody in your team.

You need to have an iron will when you are shaping your business. You can never show weakness to anybody around you, including your staff, customers, friends or family. Steve Jobs had what staff described as a 'reality distortion field' around him in that he refused to accept that things were not possible. While it upset many people along the way, and he was sometimes considered a lunatic, it also helped him to create some of the best products of all time that now define entire industries. I've worked with so many companies where decisions are made by committee and through a process. Truly great companies have one or two people who lead them and who have unshakeable resolve. People who make the decisions that clearly defy all logic and reason and are based on nothing but pure gut instinct.

In Chapter 2 I wrote about the time in Simply Zesty that we were woefully short of cash to pay the wages yet

I still signed off on a purchase order to pay for props for a video shoot. In that moment I had to look my employee in the eye, keep all my strength and in effect tell a lie and put us further into the shit.

These sorts of moments happen in a business every day in every corner of the world. You have to hold your nerve and keep reassuring people that things will be all right. Your job is to protect others from the shit that is happening and allow them to do their jobs. If the staff had known the position we were in that week there would have been a mass downing of tools and demands for explanations. When you are an entrepreneur or have your own business or team to manage you are often walking the tightest tightrope you could ever imagine, but it is absolutely imperative that you keep up a strong guard at all times and don't show weakness. That is how you get shit done and take things to the next level.

One of my projects is called Lovin' Dublin. It is essentially a guide to food in my home city. The website attracts half a million visitors a month and the traffic is growing all the time. We run events that attract tens of thousands of people every year. We now employ five people full time and the company will turn over €1 million in its second year of trading. It all seems like a massive success now but to get it to where it is today I decided to win really ugly for eighteen months before pushing the accelerate button.

Lovin' Dublin started as a blog that a friend built for me on WordPress for €700. I didn't even register the business as a limited company for eighteen months because it wasn't actually a business. We made no money whatsoever during that period because it was just me writing the blog in my spare time. I actually started it right after selling Simply Zesty as a side project for a little bit of fun. Using nothing but my own words and the camera on my iPhone, along with lots of hard work, I built that blog up to 250,000 visitors. I'd take pictures of fancy meals during business lunches and review the restaurant that night when I got home, writing until the early hours. Then I decided to start photographing my own food and providing simple recipes. Every night I'd be feeding myself a delicious meal and showing my followers how to cook it.

The audience grew through hard work, late nights and building it all in my spare time. Along the way people constantly told me to start monetizing the blog by placing ads on it or to start letting people send me free stuff to be reviewed. Given that I had just sold a business and had good contacts I would very easily have been able to raise a sneaky €100,000 and fund Lovin' Dublin properly, hiring a couple of people, getting offices and taking the quick route to making some cash. I suppose the failure of iFoods, where I'd seen that money doesn't always bring success, and the journey through Simply Zesty, where we had multiple investors, showed me that sometimes it is better to chart your own course and have nobody to answer to. Now it helped that I had some money in the bank and didn't have to worry about making a living, so I decided to bootstrap Lovin' Dublin: to slog it out and win ugly for eighteen months. The end result was that I built a business that had truly solid foundations and when it eventually got so big that I could no longer manage it on my own I held all the cards. People were emailing me and pitching me in person to let them invest in the company.

Because I'd played such a long game and built so much into the brand I could control my own destiny and choose who I wanted to join me to expand the business. I went with Irish rugby player Jamie Heaslip, who was able to add tremendous value and is the best business partner I could wish for. If I'd gone to him or others looking to raise some cash after three months with just a WordPress site and a couple of recipes I'd have been laughed out of town.

We live in a world where most start-ups assume they need to raise money to succeed. Indeed, raising cash is seen by many as the defining moment and I cringe when I see companies having extravagant launch parties to celebrate the fact that they've managed to attract investors. Venture capital can be great and it can speed things up for you but if you have a good idea and some early impetus, that is not the time to be bringing cash into the business from outside. Push it on as much as you can yourself first and sweat out every last possibility before you accept money from others. Launch with an average product and start selling it immediately. Max out your credit card and beg a few quid from friends and family. Take those first few steps in as ugly a fashion as possible; fight for the hard yards rather than going for the easy score of letting someone else fund your business. The simple reality of selling shares is that as soon as you have done so the company is no longer yours. You have ceded at least partial control to investors who will almost certainly have ideas different from yours.

When I sat up late at night editing photos for Lovin' Dublin, writing for hours while not earning a penny, it wasn't the easiest option. It was extremely painful and it would have been much less so to have taken the quick way out and involved others. But those eighteen months of pain have today given me complete control over a company I love, which is super-well funded, has the best team I could ever imagine and that has been shaped according to my vision and no one else's.

You need to win ugly if you want to get things done but, to echo another theme in this book, you simply can't do it on your own. The biggest escapes and ugliest wins all come via teamwork and having people who are willing to put their bodies or minds on the line with you. I like choosing people I admire as exemplars and there is no one in the business world today better at winning ugly than Facebook's CEO, Mark Zuckerberg. Granted, he is a programming genius who built a global brand from his laptop in a college dorm room, but it is his ability to get through the tough moments in his career and to do whatever it takes to win that should inspire us all.

While the press celebrates his many milestones – like hitting a billion users or becoming a multibillionaire after going public – it is what he does when his back is against the wall and his company is in trouble that makes him perhaps the best CEO of his generation. I can think of many occasions when, with the world against him, he did whatever it took to get his company back on track and moving onwards to greater success. Look at the move to mobile and how Facebook's revenue was being decimated as users switched to apps. First, he bet everything on becoming a mobile-first company, which took tremendous nerve when he had to stand up to Wall Street and his shareholders, forsaking the quick buck. He then paid a remarkable $19 billion for Whatsapp to eliminate a competitor, a move the history books will show was one of the smartest ever made.

In his earlier days he was willing to push the boundaries of his users' privacy to try and make the service better. Over the years he has either outperformed his competitors (Snapchat and Foursquare) or bought them out (Whatsapp, Instagram) and generally done whatever it takes to win. He has assembled a like-minded team of people around him that now numbers thousands, meaning Facebook will always stay number one in the world at what it does no matter what.

The company has had to cope with several founders, multiple lawsuits and plenty of disgruntled people along the way to success, yet still people think that this one young kid has just got lucky with an idea and some unrivalled programming skills. Mark Zuckerberg has not become the tycoon he is today, with billions of users and an incredible company, by always having things go his way. He has been in a position plenty of times during his thirty years when he has had to roll up his sleeves and win ugly, and he hasn't ever been scared to do just that.

We'd all love the world to be one big easy ride, but the reality is there are ups and downs out there when it comes to getting shit done. It might not always be right and it might not be what they teach in business books or college, but sometimes you need to win ugly to win at all.

10

Brand 'you'

Both at home and at work, branding is one of the most crucial skills you'll ever learn. Your every decision is influenced by branding: the alarm on your smartphone; the toothpaste in your bathroom; the orange juice in your fridge. Trillions of euros are spent by companies all over the world trying to build brand image, but if you think of it as something only 'the big guys' do you'll allow one of the greatest tools of business to lie unused.

I wake up in the morning thinking about brands and go to sleep at night wondering how I can improve every facet of the brands I am involved with – my own companies. What are the best ones doing? What can we do to improve ours?

From the moment we set up Simply Zesty I was obsessed with brand. I knew it could make us stand out from the hundreds of other agencies and I'd learned the trick by watching another little company in Dublin called Contrast run by two ambitious young friends called Eoghan McCabe and Des Traynor. (They now run a company called Intercom that is valued at hundreds of millions of euros in the USA.) Although just one of hundreds of website-building companies in Dublin, they stood head and shoulders above everybody else both in the calibre of work they attracted and, more importantly, in the size of the fees they charged. Boy, could they charge.

The reason was that they had distinguished themselves with incredible branding and wonderful design to make Contrast stand out from the crowd. While most web companies use stock imagery and fill their 'About us' pages with lofty technical talk the guys had their team stand by a disused garage pretending to be rock stars and lashed it up on their website in black and white. The initial reaction was 'Who the hell are these guys?' but that quickly changed as the quality of their work shone through and they distinguished themselves in a crowded marketplace. They also poured their knowledge out on their blog and were never scared to say what they thought about shoddy work from others or trends within their industry. By focusing on their own brand they were quickly able to start turning down work they didn't like, upping their prices and creating an elite image for themselves. They did a ton of different things in their time and their company will probably sell for a billion dollars pretty soon, but for me it all started with one little picture; by standing out and being different from everybody else and realizing the importance of brand.

The memory of that one picture has had a lasting influence on everything I do, and it is an outstanding example of the power of imagery and PR. Creating a brand is about being different from the crowd, doing your own thing and putting a unique spin on your product. I don't think when the lads stood up against that garage door and took a picture they had any master plan in mind, but they did know that they needed to stand out. When you are a start-up and struggling to pay the bills and meet deadlines it might seem incredibly foolish to be focusing on something as 'fluffy' as your brand because it isn't something that is going to give you an instant return. But in the long run it is crucial for getting noticed and getting shit done.

If branding can make a massive difference to small companies it can have an even bigger impact for the really big guys who have lots of time and money to spend on it. I've talked a lot about Apple in this book, and I know that as the most valuable company in the world there are many elements in their overall strategy that got them there. But for all their groundbreaking products, Steve Jobs himself, great adverts and clever marketing, I don't think they would have come anywhere close to where they are now were it not for their branding.

Apple's brand awareness and their attention to detail is summed up by their packaging. It's the first Apple product any new customer touches, and something about which Steve Jobs and Jony Ive obsessed for years. The magnetic touch to the wrapping as it peels away. The engineered perfection with which every piece slots into the perfectly square box. Have you ever noticed just how square the corners are on a new iPhone box? Do you think that is an accident? Somebody somewhere has roasted some poor designer and supplier until the edges are sharp to the point where they nearly cut you.

Everything from the way the phone charger is wrapped to the font on the instruction manual has been argued over and perfected to within an inch of its life. It's the same attention to detail you see in a Gucci shoe or when walking into a top-end restaurant.

At Apple that brand touches everything else they do. So when you walk into any of their hundreds of stores around the world you'll get that same clean look, sharp edges and minimalist feel. Watch a TV ad; enter one of their offices; visit the website. It's all about the brand. When their products appear in the coolest TV shows or the latest hip movie you probably think that has happened by chance but it actually comes from their brand team. I've dealt with Apple a couple of times as a supplier and when working with some of their clients, and the instructions they send out on how their brand should be used on third-party sites are about as anal as it gets. Nothing is left to chance. No edge must be too rounded; no iPhone blurred. The consumer could touch the brand in any one of thousands of ways, but when they do so it should always be the same Apple-branded experience.

This is the very top end of the scale and Apple get it so right that they have nearly turned their brand into a religion whose faithful queue for days in advance to get their hands on the latest offering. It is not a phone or a tablet computer that people are buying, but an experience.

By focusing on their brand so intensely they have created millions of brand 'advocates' around the world. People like you and me who love the Apple brand so much that we have effectively become the biggest sales force in the world. I'd say a hundred people have purchased Apple products because of my recommendations. That is happening all over the world right now and that is all down to the strategic importance they put on their brand. If Apple can become a global giant with ridiculous profits by focusing on brand, it shows that it could pay for you too when it comes to making money and getting shit done.

I'm seen by some as a social media guru and the guy who knows everything about the online world, and food in particular. That hasn't happened overnight and it hasn't happened by accident. I've actually worked very hard on my brand over the years to get it to a point where people can define in a couple of words what my brand is and what I stand for. As soon as I walk into a room in Dublin people I don't know will say, 'Ah, you're that social media guy,' or, 'You are the guy who knows all about online marketing.' Think of some of the people you know who are getting shit done and you'll instantly be able to pigeonhole them as 'the butcher' or 'the microbrewer' or 'the designer'.

From the moment I made that first internet video on the yacht I was destined to become what I am. I had no idea at the time what I wanted to be or where the journey would lead me, but it has taken all of seven years to become that person, so the sooner you start to create your own brand, the better. Begin by writing down exactly what you want to be. The aim could be as simple as an English teacher in your local school or as ambitious as the news anchor on national TV. Once you have decided where you want to go, you can start to take practical steps to get there.

In the early days of Simply Zesty, though I was heading up a creative agency, I started wearing suits in an attempt to fit into the new corporate world I now inhabited. One day I was waiting to go into a pitch meeting with a large multinational client. Another agency was attending the briefing and I sniggered to myself when I saw their creative director slouched in a chair wearing a baseball cap and scribbling notes on a jotter. When I saw that, I knew we had the business in the bag.

As the meeting progressed I thought things were going pretty well. The guy in the cap didn't say a word and as far as I could tell he was dead and buried. Then, halfway through, just as I presumed we were about to get the work, he started talking about social media and digital campaigns. His knowledge was no deeper than mine and he wasn't saying anything especially remarkable but suddenly all the suits in the room sat up. They were mesmerized by his every word. As I tried to interrupt I was literally shushed as we all listened to this chap telling us about the future. After he'd finished, he went back to doodling on his pad and ignored us for the rest of the meeting.

A couple of weeks later I found out that we didn't get the €50,000 contract and the other agency had won it. I knew immediately that it was all down to the guy in the baseball cap, but why? Then it dawned on me that he was selling something different – ideas, something that nobody in a suit could ever deliver – and that they believed he had a magic wand that could take them to places they had no idea existed. The day we lost that contract I went into town and changed my dress style once and for all. I wasn't happy wearing a suit anyway and felt a bit of a fraud doing so. I bought trainers, hats, hoodies, quirky T-shirts and all the other stuff I had been used to wearing before my new business career.

From that moment on I walked into client meetings dressed like an overgrown teenager. I met CEOs and executives of large companies and their attitude towards me changed instantly. I was lucky enough to be thirty then and have twenty people working for me and I could instantly see them thinking, *God, this guy walks in here dressed like that and doesn't seem fazed by us; he must really know a load of shit we don't know.* I've never seen chequebooks open quicker in my life. In a suit, I was simply a poorer version of what they were, but with a quirky hat and some mad ideas I'd suddenly acquired something they couldn't understand and something that they simply had to pay top dollar for. I have so much to thank that guy wearing the baseball cap for because he taught me the biggest lesson in branding ever, and that was not to pretend to be something that you are not.

While Apple have always been strong on the design side of things, that isn't true of all companies. For its first decade Google didn't place much emphasis on design, preferring to produce functional products that had clearly been 'designed' by engineers. Then Apple showed the world that good design was not only enjoyed by niche groups but could also help shift more product and make a company wildly profitable by increasing what people were willing to pay for it. Many of the biggest and fastest growing companies – from Google and Facebook through to Square and Airbnb – now place tremendous emphasis on design. The standard of online design is now so high that if there is a direct battle between two companies design could be the deciding factor.

Ryanair, one of the most successful airlines on the planet, for years were happy to push users through a horrendously designed yellow monstrosity of a website that was like a minefield in terms of avoiding costs and being tricked into buying stuff you didn't want. The reason Ryanair didn't change it was because it was working and none of their competitors was doing anything better. But as soon as some better-designed options came along and profits started to dip, the airline quickly overhauled the website with a slick new look. Ryanair were forced to change suddenly because consumers were moving to something that was giving them a much better experience. Consumers will put up with bad design and branding if there are no other options available but what we are starting to see all over the world is that customers pick the best-designed stuff. Design-led companies are becoming the norm rather than the exception nowadays.

That change is especially evident when it comes to mobile technology as a whole new world emerges. The early attempts at mobile design were essentially miniaturized desktop websites but that isn't the solution for this new platform. A large monitor, a mouse and a keyboard provide a completely different experience from a small touch screen. It's clear that PCs and laptops are on the decline and that the future will be mobile. And mobile won't be used alongside traditional computers but instead of them. People in the developing world coming to the internet for the first time will be buying a mobile or a tablet, as will future generations in the West. Many people will never own what we call a computer today.

Every business must focus on design and especially on the mobile space if they don't want to be caught with their pants down. The good news is that, as with any disruptive technology, there is massive opportunity there for those who embrace it. If you want to get shit done either personally, professionally or in any walk of life then get thinking very seriously about design and mobile.

Do you ever walk into a supermarket and wonder why you are paying nearly double what you'd be charged down the road?

This is another example of branding, because although not everybody will pay twice the going rate for the weekly shop there are many who are happy to pay a little extra for what is perceived – rightly or wrongly – as a better-quality product. Why, for example, would you pay double for a bunch of carrots in a supermarket a hundred yards from a cheaper one? It might be because the dearer carrots are washed and nicely wrapped in little bundles as opposed to being loose in a dirty crate on the floor, or that the staff greet you with a smile, or that they've paid for a lovely bespoke sign with slick design. Perhaps the background music is that little bit better and when you check out there is no queue and the bags are paper instead of plastic, which you know is better for the environment. The carrots might be identical, but people are always willing to pay more for stuff that is nicely branded and that is something you could be using to your advantage.

We did it in Simply Zesty and I was amazed at how positive an effect pricing can have when it comes to building your brand. We had a set day rate of €600 for our services at the foundation of the company, which was serving us well and making us money. As soon we appointed Ken as our CEO he said that we should increase that rate to €1,000. I was terrified we'd lose all our clients and never win a piece of business again because all our competitors were now cheaper than us, but when we went ahead with the price increase the most remarkable thing happened. Business started flooding through the door, our existing clients gave us more work and we earned a new level of respect. We'd quickly moved up the value chain in the eyes of a number of our clients and, rather than losing work as I had feared, we drastically improved our brand and our image.

In the early days of Simply Zesty we'd been focused on

making sales in the €3–5,000 range, and although we were good at them they were always hard work. What I saw as our prices rose was that it was actually a good deal easier to make a sale of €50,000 than it was one of €5,000. With the lower price, clients would be scrutinizing every little detail and making sure they were getting value for money while still trying to beat us down. When we moved up to the higher value range and started pitching work at what we thought were crazy prices I saw people saying yes all the time. Not only were we doing the same amount of work for a sale ten times the size but the people we were selling to weren't even questioning the price and were signing off a lot quicker. I learned so much about pricing in that period as it showed me that people like paying for quality. Not everybody will pay the higher price, but one way of getting a lot of shit done is to double your prices, no matter what it is that you are selling.

Good branding is vital to any start-up. It's the first thing I concentrated on at PR Slides because I knew it was the quickest way to make us a global force, to earn more sales and help us through future large fund-raising rounds. But what does branding look like on the ground in a start-up and how do you start making it happen? Well, the truth is it comprises hundreds of different things done on an ongoing basis. Some are long term, but there are also some you can address quickly and easily that will have an almost instant impact:

1. Design

I don't care how small your company is or how little cash you have; unless you are a designer yourself you need some sort of design help. Hire somebody within your budget (you can get a student for a couple of hundred euros). Get them to create a universal look that can be applied to everything you do: your website, logo, office branding, social media profiles and anything connected to you in the real world. These are the points at which people will first encounter your brand so it needs to look incredible, but more than anything it needs to be unified and instantly recognizable as belonging to you.

2. Business cards and email signatures

Every email you send is an interaction with your brand. A good logo, links to websites and title will establish your brand and start making you seem bigger than you are. If you've followed my advice in point 1 customers will be engaging with you across multiple platforms and thinking what a large and professional business you're running. Business cards are the same: a tiny piece of your brand that you are giving people to take home with them. It should be perfect and contain leads to all the places you'd like them to go, such as your website or Twitter feed.

3. Office culture

If you are lucky enough to have an office and a few employees you will need to think seriously about office culture. Does the place look good? Do you have strong branding everywhere? Can all the staff have a beer together on a Friday? You should buy ice creams when it's sunny outside. Remember that the staff of your company should be your biggest brand advocates and having them out there singing the praises of what you do is vitally important for your brand.

4. Photos and video

Previous generations would have had to spend a fortune on producing video or photo content but because of the advances in technology this couldn't really be any cheaper these days. Shooting a simple promo video and getting some slick photos for your business shouldn't cost much more than €1,000, and if done right it can create the impression that you are a lot bigger than you are. It's the sort of thing only sizeable companies used to be able to do but now anybody can create wonderful rich media content for a snip.

These are just some of the quick wins that you can apply when starting to build your brand. (They are just as relevant on a personal level, too.) In reality your brand embraces everything from the cleaner who vacuums your carpet right through to the furnishings approved by your

CEO for an office makeover. Social media lets you craft a brand incredibly cheaply these days, but it won't happen all by itself. You need to work on it and build it from the ground up. You could be a tiny local cafe or a company the size of Apple, but to get shit done you need a better brand, so get to work on it right now.

I find it interesting to look at how brands in creative industries are built up. Take the music business as an example, acknowledged worldwide as the hardest industry to crack. There are millions of young people trying to become global superstars but, of course, only a handful will ever make it. So what is the difference between four guys belting out tunes to six mates in the local pub and a band whose brand sells out stadia all over the world and who have a six- or seven-figure fan-base. It could be that they're better musicians (although plenty would disagree), but the reality is branding.

Coldplay, probably the most successful band in the world, also has the best brand right now. There is a uniformity that runs through all the band's activities. To see a Coldplay gig is to feel the brand. The shooting coloured lasers around the stage; the coloured bracelets given out at concerts that synchronize with the music; the T-shirts; the clothes the members of the band wear; the promotional material that first attracted you to the gig and the videos you watch on the band's beautifully branded YouTube channel after the gig. All this focuses on one thing: Chris Martin's multi-coloured piano, from which every other element of the Coldplay brand derives. This isn't just a band but rather a brand. Coldplay has identified what it is good at and made its brand icon the focal point of the show.

An incredible Coldplay gig might prompt me to follow them on social media channels, listen to their music on Spotify or download an album. And although the content is available both across the internet and in the high street, the brand is uniformly perfect no matter what the platform. With each click, each download, each video, each purchase I become more immersed in the brand and start sharing it with and championing it to others. Yes, you need a lot of talent to become the world's best-loved band, but more than anything you need incredible branding.

Another trick used by both Coldplay and U2 is to label themselves 'the biggest band in the world'. They've each done that for years, though I believe U2 were first, and it is an incredibly smart piece of branding. Is it true? Nobody really knows or cares, but it plants the seed in the head of consumers. Who wouldn't be attracted to 'the biggest band in the world coming to a stadium near you'? Both bands are huge, of course, but the important factor is that they had the balls to make the claim whether it was true or not, and to project that image regardless. That's what has kept these guys at the top for so long.

So even if you are a tiny hip-hop act or a movie maker trying to get funding for your first film, you need to be thinking about your brand. It isn't the only reason

Coldplay are where they are today but it is one of the biggest. There are now hundreds of people all over the world employed to promote their brand, but in the early days it was established by the lads themselves. They were the ones who built the Coldplay brand into what it has become today. If you want to get shit done and stand out, start working on your brand.

I've spoken at over 300 events in the last five years, ranging from major international conferences with thousands of attendees to modest gatherings of about a dozen people wanting to learn about social media or marketing. I live by one simple rule when it comes to speaking at events and building my brand: I'll turn up absolutely anywhere I can get hold of a microphone. I rarely charge, and then only for travelling expenses to a far-flung location. There is no more powerful way to build your brand than being the onstage 'expert'. Whatever field you start off in, be it car parking or genetic engineering, you are no more an expert than anybody else, but as soon as you walk onto a stage, sit on a panel or chair a discussion you are instantly lifted to another level.

The first couple of times I was asked to speak were almost accidental. I just happened to know a lot about social media and was fairly vocal on Twitter. I was a bag of nerves as I stood before a group of forty people and gave my thoughts about the emergence of Twitter, Facebook and YouTube and how they could change the world. When I'd finished, though, I found something amazing happening as audience members asked me for help with their business, advice on their own issues or just general questions about where I thought social media might be heading. I'd walked in a nobody and now, simply because I'd taken a few hours to throw some slides together and give a talk to forty people, I was in demand as an 'expert'. Your content has to be good and you can't bullshit to a crowd, but there is no better way to build your own personal brand than by holding a microphone and talking about the subject you know most about. As in most fields, the initial breakthrough is key. Once you have given a couple of talks others will soon follow and you'll soon be known as an expert.

So the theory is good, but how do you land an invitation to speak? The first way is pretty straightforward . . . just ask. You don't get anything without asking and if you hear of a conference, event or gathering to which you think you could add value then start connecting with the organizer. As anybody who organizes events will tell you, finding speakers can be tough, so if you pitch them correctly and show that you can improve their event they might well agree.

Another simple trick is to have a 'public speaking' section on your website or blog that includes a picture of you and some information about the subjects you cover. Post the slides or videos you plan to use in your presentations there as well. Make yourself look professional and experienced and – crucially – make it easy for people to contact you via email or phone. A strong personal presence on the web is a great way to gain speaking engagements. If you publish amazing content that you are proud of, conference organizers will soon be asking you to share it with their audiences.

There is a final technique which is guaranteed to work brilliantly but which involves even more effort. Organize an event yourself, based on your own area of expertise. Appoint a few other speakers and either give yourself a slot or chair the entire thing. Event organizers are usually rewarded with a greatly elevated profile and access to some of the brightest and smartest minds out there. It's a lot of work but it's highly effective.

As we discussed in the chapter on technology, if you want to start a business you have a vast array of tools at your fingertips and most of them are absolutely free to use. Unfortunately you will be up against dozens if not hundreds of direct competitors with access to the same resources. It doesn't matter whether you are a small organic wine maker or a multinational insurance provider, you are going to have to stand out to get ahead. Although the technology may be new and using it involves learning about video production and social-media advertising and so on, what it all boils down to is whether you are able to tell a good story. Storytelling is the oldest form of marketing in the world and, when done correctly, leads to the most powerful type of business or personal lead: effective word-of-mouth recommendation. Social media and other new technologies have placed word-of-mouth marketing on steroids. One satisfied customer in your restaurant used to tell a handful of people about the experience, but social media allows a positive (or negative) experience to be instantly relayed along with a photo to hundreds or thousands of people.

So, to start building your own personal or company brand you need to find your own story. What makes you unique? What makes you stand out from the hundreds of other companies operating in your space or the other 7 billion people on the planet? You need to identify what makes you interesting and often that can be the human angle. Maybe you have an extraordinary passion for something. If you love wine, for example, talk about it, share photos, tweets, videos or blog posts on an ongoing basis and you'll eventually build that brand. Talk non-stop about wine and demonstrate your expertise to anybody who'll listen, and even though at the moment you're an accounts clerk doing a job you hate you are taking the first steps towards telling your story and building your brand. Your future is a blank canvas, so start thinking about what you want it to look like.

If good branding lets you charge more, attract and retain more customers as well as making you more valuable personally and professionally, then clearly we should all be doing more of it. It is too easy to brush off branding as a 'nice to have' or 'something I'll do when I have some spare time'. Too many businesses and individuals fail to get shit done and stagnate, not fulfilling their true potential simply because they don't aim high enough or think about building a brand. They build what they think is a good business but they don't focus on how branding could turn it into a brilliant one.

With Lovin' Dublin I took a unique approach, ignoring the business aspect of it for the first eighteen months and instead putting every ounce of energy I had into building it into a brand. On a practical level that meant focusing purely on the quality of design. Making sure that every one of the photos was absolutely perfect and fitted exactly the template that I'd devised on day one. That every font I used was perfectly aligned. That all my staff fitted in with the brand and understood it from day one.

See, there are hundreds of food blogs based in Ireland, and thousands around the world, but I needed to create a brand to help mine stand out. Because I focused not on making money but only on building the brand, the site now has 400,000 people visiting it every month. They all feel part of the brand and as the journey has continued we haven't had to spend a penny on advertising because those people have become our advocates, just like Apple's customers, recommending our product to their friends and spreading the word. The Lovin' Dublin brand is now so strong that the tiniest change to the site's ethos has people writing emails and comments giving out about it. I find ongoing negative feedback to be one of the biggest indicators that you have something good. Much worse to have something so average that nobody can be bothered to give any feedback at all.

While feedback is important for your brand, you should not act on it all. Use it to inform your decisions about branding and design by all means, but always build the brand that *you* want and not the one others have in mind for you. As Henry Ford said, 'If I'd asked my customers what they wanted they would have said a faster horse.'

While Lovin' Dublin is no more than a website at the moment, it is a brand in my head. In years to come you'll be able to touch it in the real world, interact with it at live events and experience it the same way you experience an iPad or a can of Coca-Cola. To many that still sounds very fluffy, and they will question where the missing revenue might come from, but my aim is to create a luxury brand that people will be passionate about. I'll then have future pricing power and a route to phenomenal profits. There may be thousands of food websites out there, but there are very few brands as distinctive as Lovin' Dublin, and the work I am putting in now will help me get some phenomenal shit done in the future.

Start thinking today of ways to put time, money and energy into improving your brand and design. It is one of the most effective tools available when it comes to creating long-term value.

11

Happiness is knowing the stuff that really counts

Getting shit done is not about making money. I admit that might sound glib coming from a guy who has bought a house, sold a business, published a book and drives a slick car. I remember other people who had sold businesses or inherited a fortune saying money wasn't all that important and thinking, *What an asshole, of course it is!* Now I think wealth is the most bullshit metric there has ever been.

If you find something you're good at and really love doing you might make more money than you could ever imagine, but as a measure of happiness, money is an empty number. It is a useful tool and it helps you get functional stuff done like hiring a cleaner or taking fancy holidays, but it does not transform you or bring you contentment. I was nearly at my most unhappy after selling my business, even though being rich had always been my dream, something I thought would make all my other problems simply disappear. Sure, wouldn't all girls love me if I had money, and I'd be able to eat healthy food all day instead of drinking? I'd be able to sit on a warm beach doing yoga and finally get rid of my panic attacks. But after all the partying, when I looked at my newly healthy bank balance and realized not a thing about me had changed, I suddenly got more worried and more depressed and drank even more heavily to escape my problems.

I'd swap every penny I have right now not to have panic attacks, to meet a nice girl and surf all day in Hawaii. Do you think when I am on my deathbed coughing up my last breath I'll remember the ridiculous €1,500 watch I bought when I was twenty-three in the Bahamas after getting a big tip? Do you think I'll remember the Gucci suit I bought for €2,000 and wore five times when I was young and trying to be flash? No, I'll be thinking about that stunning girl I dated in Antigua who I'd thought was way out of my league, or the time I rode the freshest powder down the side of a mountain in France with Sean, screaming at the top of my voice from equal measures of exhilaration and panic. Experiences, not acquisitions, are what we value most.

I'd wanted a dog since I was about eight years old. First, my dad said no and then when I was older, working in kitchens, living on boats or in small apartments and slogging it out in start-ups meant it was never possible. As we approached the sale of Simply Zesty I started to think about getting a dog again. Six months before selling I changed my computer wallpaper to a picture of a dog. It was my life's ambition and at thirty-two I thought it might now just be possible, even though there was a lot still to do. Although my mind and body were shattered, and the stress of running a growing business was taking its toll, when I logged in every day and saw my future pet I pushed that little bit harder. Sometimes getting shit done is just about having the right incentive. I bought the dog, and it remains my proudest personal achievement. Snoop cost me €150 and it is easily the best €150 I have ever spent. When I go climbing on a Sunday morning, hangover free, with Snoop bobbing along behind with a big doggy smile on his face and his tongue out, that's one of the times I realize what it truly means to get shit done. I got an even better deal on my second dog, Buster. A friend found him abandoned in a park and I said I'd take him in for a week until we found him a home. Of course he is still with me. I love them both dearly.

In his iconic book *Outliers*, Malcolm Gladwell wrote that it takes 10,000 hours to really become an expert at anything. Although that book was published as recently as 2008, I'm not sure that rule applies any more. Not in the new world we live in where companies like Instagram can be built into $1 billion businesses within two years. Not in a world where young people might have five different careers before they are thirty and find one they settle into. The world is changing and we all need to develop as broad a suite of skills as possible. Journalists need to know how to design, TV producers need to know about internet marketing and taxi drivers need to know how to use the latest smartphone apps to pick up fares.

So if we all need multiple skills, what metrics can we put in place to make sure we are focusing on the right thing and not doing a load of irrelevant stuff? Well, if one metric has served me well over the years it is consistency. The best restaurants in the world are not the ones who serve one flamboyantly brilliant meal followed by a dud. A good sports team is consistent and grinds out results in an ugly fashion when needed. The key to getting shit done is being metronomically consistent in what you do and keeping the standards as high as you possibly can.

Take my blogging over the years. When I did it in iFoods, Simply Zesty and now in PR Slides and Lovin' Dublin, I may not always have had the best content going, but I never went a day without posting something. Sometimes with a bruising hangover or while being floored by flu it would have been easier to say, 'Ah forget about it, I'll get back to it tomorrow,' and let it slip, but I always stayed consistent. Being consistent isn't sexy and it doesn't win you praise in the short term, but if you keep working hard, doing the same thing well and staying focused you will find that it is the best metric you can ever apply. It doesn't matter if you are a road bike racer, a dog trainer or one of the world's best CEOs, if you manage to incorporate consistency into what you do you'll eventually grind out the shit that you want to get done. Once you've done that it is usually just a matter of time before you achieve the things you want to.

On my first weekend in a professional kitchen I had to cook eggs Benedict, a technically challenging dish that involves poaching eggs, making the tricky sauce hollandaise and bringing together several different items with precision timing to create a flawless dish. I remember clearly that I had fourteen plates returned to the kitchen and as a green eighteen-year-old I felt like crying and giving it all up there and then. Every time another order came in my heart sank a little. My eggs were all over the place, the sauce would be splitting and I was digging myself a deeper hole by the day.

For the next week I read everything I could about the dish. I asked other chefs to show me tricks. I watched people making it. The following week I wasn't that much better but I had improved. When I was in college I'd teach myself how to poach eggs perfectly while the others listened to theory classes. Eventually, after about five weeks of taking a beating on breakfast service, I mastered it. Finally I could hold my own and that skill has stayed with me ever since. Now anytime I make eggs Benedict I know it will be absolutely perfect and wonderfully consistent.

Consistency means getting up when the alarm sounds instead of hitting snooze. It means forgoing the fancy coffee and saving €2.50 a day. It means opening the laptop and writing lines of code until you know how to build a website. Not being scared to fail, immersing yourself in the challenge – be it cooking the perfect eggs Benedict or learning how to play the piano – is key. I found that once something had been learned it became as simple as the song 'Eat, Sleep, Rave, Repeat'. So to get shit done, focus as hard as you can on consistency. Once you have that, everything else is a formality.

*

My panic attacks were so bad at one stage that I thought I'd die pretty soon. On one occasion a friend and I sat at home and decided we would make some hash cookies. I hadn't smoked weed in about a year and he never smoked it but work had been stressful and we just took a notion. I was off booze at the time and feeling especially stressed, and had decided we needed to get off our heads in some way or another. To make a long story short, I ate three of them and after an hour, in a matter of minutes, went from feeling fabulously high to having a complete meltdown. I lost control of my body and slumped to the floor. I was shaking desperately and my legs were like jelly. All I could hear out of my mouth was 'I'm going to need an ambulance'. As I sat there in another world I could hear my friend on the phone in the background. *This isn't good*, I thought. I was both out of it and very aware at the same time.

In that moment everything became clear. I mean everything. I didn't think once about billable hours or what innovative smartphone I should buy to impress people. I didn't think about how many euros I had in my bank account or the bigger TV I wanted. All I could think about was the look I could imagine on my dad's face. Thank God my good friend was there with me. Every vivid detail about all the things I had failed to do in my life starting hitting me. The mistakes I'd made with girls I should have looked after better. The things I said no to because I was too scared. As we whizzed down the motorway with sirens blaring and the paramedic hooking me up to an ECG, between prayers I contemplated death and vowed to never waste another hour in my life.

In St Vincent's the ambulance driver took us in and I was wheeled into the emergency room. When I told them what I'd taken they thought I was lying and had overdosed on coke or something far more serious, but with six doctors around me poking wires into me and carrying out all sorts of tests I had a moment of absolute clarity. One day this would be for real. Today I was just a gobshite who had failed to look after his body, worked too hard and taken too much weed, but one day – it could be tomorrow or when I'm forty or when I'm eighty – I would be breathing my last and I didn't want to have the regrets I'd had when lying there at twenty-nine.

It turned out I was suffering from nothing more serious than an extremely bad panic attack that had been exaggerated by the vast amount of weed in my bloodstream. The doctors dosed me up with Valium. When I woke up ten hours later on a trolley I was surrounded by people who had been in car crashes or industrial accidents and were genuinely at death's door. I got straight up and, although having possibly the worst 'stoneover' known to man, and not knowing left from right, I checked myself out. I thanked the doctors and walked home and said, 'That's it, never again.'

I rested up and vowed to get more important shit done and not waste another second. There is nothing like the clarity of a near-death experience (or a panic attack that makes you imagine one) to focus the mind and that night something fundamental changed for me.

Most of us start the day with some sort of to-do list. It might be an online reminder, an app, written on a piece of paper or stored in our head. We even start the year like this, scribbling down fanciful resolutions that are never kept. But the simple fact is that most of us fail miserably in getting the shit done that we want to. We use crazy metrics. Is our email inbox empty? Have we hit the quarterly targets? Do we have the 7-series BMW instead of the 5-series in the neighbour's driveway? As I've said, the vast majority of our metrics are based around future goals (graduating from college, making partner or retiring) which are predominantly financially based, or are the metrics that other people have given us that have been there for generations. Getting shit done is all about flipping those metrics and trying to establish a set that will create real meaning in your life and make you achieve the things you have always dreamed of.

So instead of thinking about billable hours or engine size, why not use metrics such as the number of days off work you can get this year while maintaining your standard of living, or how you can decrease the amount of time you spend on email from five hours a day to one. How many cakes can you bake in a week? Research whatever really matters to you and chase those metrics instead of trying to keep up with the Joneses and the things your neighbours think are important.

One again I'll use Lovin' Dublin as an example. There is such an engaged and passionate community there and enough traffic there for me to flip the business, just sell advertising and make a really quick buck. I could hire staff, keep their wages low and slap advertising all over the site, making enough to take a step back and live on the beach in Miami. Instead, my goals are to provide something amazing for Dubliners and put a smile on people's faces. Sure, I need it to make money and cover the wages of the staff, but instead of getting a few quick euros for a banner ad I get far more satisfaction from hundreds of people opening up one of our hand-delivered food boxes and being blown away by the ingredients. That makes an Irish restaurant happy, it pays for people to be employed in my company and brightens the day for hundreds of people.

My main metrics for Lovin' Dublin are fun and brand building. So while I focus on those, bringing my dogs to the office, creating jobs that people love and maintaining a passionate community, I'm building an insane amount of value into the company by following my own metrics, not the ones the industry has defined for me. The worst-case scenario is that it doesn't work, and although that would be painful for the people working there it's a risk worth taking, because the best-case scenario is that we have an awful lot of fun along the way every single day and we create something of immense value to us all.

I think it's vital to have role models and people who influence your life. It might be somebody you know, such as a business peer, a friend or a family member, but I find famous people and people who have achieved stuff that we can only dream of are better candidates. My own hero is Ayrton Senna, the greatest racing driver and one of the most remarkable people who ever lived.

I watched him race at the top of his career in his iconic McLaren. I watched him stand up to bullies, pushing himself to the limit when others were willing to take the easy option and settle for second place. It sounds ridiculous because I'm in no way religious or even that much of a car enthusiast, but when I watched him race around the streets of Monaco I felt the closest I ever have to believing there might be a god on earth. Senna said that being in a car was the only time he could forget about everything else and just live in the moment. Not everybody will understand the analogy, but Senna at Monaco, brushing the barriers at full speed in the rain, summarizes what I want my life to be. An exhilarating series of laps with perfect consistency where not even the tiniest part of you countenances failure.

The moment I truly fell in love with Senna and decided to hold him up as my idol was when I watched a documentary about him. Following a crash, one of his fellow drivers was slumped unconscious in the cockpit in the middle of the track with cars speeding towards him at 200 mph. As Senna flew past he immediately recognized the seriousness of the situation, slammed on the brakes and jumped out of his car, risking his own life to sprint down the track to help his colleague. To be like Senna, rushing down the track, arms waving in the air with no regard for his own life, is my dream. Forgetting about the past. Forgetting about plans. Forgetting about pay increases or retirement but just living in that one moment and being true to myself.

To remind me of what he achieved I keep him close at all times. In my house I have a life-size portrait of him above the fireplace in my sitting room. I have one of his quotes tattooed on my side: 'If you no longer go for a gap that exists you are no longer a racing driver.' Every morning I look in the bathroom mirror and see those words marching across my body. In the same way that Apple employees are still asking 'What would Steve have done?' long after he died, it reminds me to be pushing the boundaries constantly and never to go for the easy option and back away from something I believe in. Of course, I'm never ever going to be the equal of Ayrton Senna, but aspiring to think like he did and live my life to the full serves me well.

Getting shit done in your own life might mean something as trivial as taking that extra exam or being captain of the sports team, but whatever goals you have will be easier to reach if you have a good role model. Our heroes set the bar, the unfeasibly high standards. You might achieve only 10 per cent of what they did, but without constantly thinking about them and the standards they set you wouldn't even have got that far. Senna is my role model because he was pig-headed about certain things and could have made easier decisions, he did what he believed was right and always went for the gap. If he was in any way conscious when he was being airlifted to hospital for the last time, I don't think he could have been even a tiny bit upset with the life he had led, despite it lasting just thirty-four years. He is my hero and in order to get shit done we should all have somebody like that in our lives, driving us on and acting as our inspiration.

I remember walking down the road with my best friend Sean when I was sixteen. I'd drunk a bottle of vodka and smoked a shitload of weed. I remember kicking wing mirrors off the car doors one by one. Sean was also pissed but he had enough sense to push me against a wall and threaten to deck me unless I stopped. We scrapped around and then finally sat down. I remember the moment precisely and slurring to him that by the time I was thirty I'd sell a business for millions. We hugged it out and started crying. I made him promise that if ever we were broken men and addicted to heroin and out on the street we'd be there for each other no matter what. I know it was just a comment in passing for him but deep down inside me I already knew that he would have to be there for me one day in that very capacity. I might have been only sixteen but I think I already knew I was an alcoholic with the capacity to self-destruct. I knew I had the ability to influence people and qualities that could help me create wealth, but I also knew that the flipside of my personality was that I'd never be far from falling to pieces.

We are all excellent at lying to ourselves, as I did for

over fifteen years before I admitted I needed counselling and that even things like making money and achieving my professional dreams were never going to make me happy. For you it could be the unhappy relationship in which you've been treated like shit for years. The dead-end job that you have never been happy doing. The simmering addiction to something that will probably kill you. We all have demons that eat away at us as we lie our way through life, not wanting to admit our failings to other people but most importantly never admitting them to ourselves.

Now that you are approaching the end of the book, I want you to do one thing for yourself. Put the book or e-reader down, find yourself a quiet corner and close your eyes. Take ten or fifteen minutes and figure out what it is that you really want to get done. What is the stuff that you have been lying to yourself about for all these years? Don't worry about how you will achieve it or what steps you have to take to get there; just take time to yourself and ask: *What shit do I want to get done?*

Go!

At work, most of us are faced with a set of targets or objectives that we must meet in order to either keep our job or gain promotion. It is how the business world functions, and although the system has flaws many businesses work very well indeed using such metrics as reports and spreadsheets. That works in our professional lives, so why not establish something similar in our personal lives? A set of business-style metrics that define us as a person and help us get personal shit done. I keep my own spread-sheet for life that is for my eyes only, and although I won't share the specific metrics I use, the principle is something you should apply. Think about achievements you could measure on a monthly, quarterly or annual basis. What metrics match your goals?

Choose goals that are reachable in the short to medium term (one to five years) and, as in business, choose metrics that *you* want rather than what other people prescribe. For example, your spreadsheet might contain a column for each month and row variables such as:

Times I tasted salt on my lips on a beach
Days spent entirely offline
Days I have been sober
Home cooked meals for my family
Girls I've kissed
Books I've read
Hours spent playing team sport
Countries I have visited

My own personal spreadsheet has twenty such variables (though not these). People who know me will tell you how poor I am at processing or keeping records, but I do find it very easy to maintain this master spreadsheet of my life. You'll find that you don't need to look at it every day, and I often don't fill mine in for a couple of weeks, but over time you'll slowly start noticing that the same processes that work in business can be a highly effective way to get more out of your life. Don't bog yourself down, because life will then suddenly feel like work, but a lightweight simple reporting tool that only you have access to can drastically improve the amount of shit you'll get done.

I've been as clear and honest as I can in this book, trying to spell out some of the things that have helped me to get my shit done. I'm acutely aware that I am a half-mad, risk-taking lunatic, but I do hope that, despite all my faults, some people will be able to pick out a few nuggets and get their own shit done. I wrote this book because I think success in both business and life is far too often dressed up in some lofty set of principles or unrealistic techniques that most people simply can't relate to.

Recall my blog post from Chapter 2: 'I am publishing a book, it will be in shops in nine months and it will be a bestseller.' I posted that nine months before writing these very words and submitting this book to the publisher. I say that not to bang my own drum but to show I am following my own advice, and that it works. I'm thirty-four years of age and have travelled the world, sold a business, cooked for billionaires and celebrities and have a couple of fast-growing businesses. I've now published a book. I've got my own house. A couple of dogs. Enough to live on comfortably for the foreseeable future. Most people would be happy with that but I want to keep setting the bar even higher. Getting more shit done.

When I sold Simply Zesty quite a few people said that I'd been lucky to be in the right place at the right time. Just as I did after iFoods failed, I screen grabbed every one of those messages. Even though they have long been forgotten by others, I look at them whenever things are tough in the businesses and I have another challenge to overcome. They drive me on. I have bigger enemies now whom I use to push me on to bigger goals. I don't mind saying publicly that I plan to sell both my businesses at some point. PR Slides will be sold for tens of millions one day as a global image resource and Lovin' Dublin will fetch millions further down the line as one of the most amazing brands that money can buy. Those two sales will have nothing to do with luck and everything to do with brutal consistency, getting up earlier than my competitors, being less scared of failure, backing people around me when they are down and doing all the other simple things that have worked for me to date. I've recently discovered a new business motto – 'Once you are lucky, twice you are good' – and I've decided to put my own addition to it: 'three times and there can be no more fucking doubt!'

I've a list of places to go and things to do that is longer than my arm and I have that list in a very public place where I can see it and be reminded of it every day. All that stuff is the easy shit to get done, though. What I really want to focus on, and what you need to tackle first, is the stuff you are lying to yourself about. Your demons. I'm not there yet in terms of getting over depression and sorting out my drinking, but every day that I admit stuff like that to myself and seek help is a day towards achieving a more balanced life and getting the really important stuff done.

I've also taken into consideration the notion that money isn't an important metric, and incorporated my love of dogs into my plans. I've decided that if I am lucky enough to be here on my fortieth birthday I'll stop working and open a canine sanctuary in Ireland. I'll pump all the money I have into it and make it a not-for-profit business. My lofty ambition for the place will be that once it is opened, no dog on the island of Ireland will ever be mistreated or have to be put down. It won't make me rich, but it will mean that I'll be able to use the business acumen I have to create something that will make the world a better place. And when I am on my deathbed breathing my last, I won't have a care in the world apart from wondering where I am going to next.

My last job on a yacht was aboard a fifty-metre boat owned by an elderly couple worth a few billion. The woman was a kind-hearted old soul who took the crew out to dinner all over the Caribbean on each island that we visited so we could create incredible memories of our own while working and being away from our families. I think she liked our company because her husband was wheelchair bound and had Alzheimer's. In Barbados she told me the husband and I were going up to Sandy Lane, which is one of the most exclusive golf resorts in the world. She'd organized for me to hit some golf balls on the driving range and her husband sat there in his wheel-chair watching me and smiling along and offering the odd word of advice on my swing. Here I was, a young chef, being made to feel like a million dollars playing golf in a location I could only dream of, having every shot cheered on by a retired billionaire. I've always remembered that, and tried to keep that sort of fun element alive for all my employees. Life is about more than work and you have to treat people decently.

The billionaire had his own private nurse to bathe and dress him and he never said much apart from laughing along with jokes and muttering to his wife. She did everything for him, including ordering his dinner and counting out his pills. He'd once been a proud mogul who had built bridges all across China and had his own business empire. It was sad to see him in this state but he still enjoyed his life, sitting at the back of the boat eating lobster and laughing to himself. When I told his wife I was leaving to start iFoods she made a big fuss, wished me all the best and took us all out to dinner. We had a few drinks and everybody came back to the boat. I was heading below deck for my last night on board before catching a flight back to Europe and the exciting but scary prospect of starting my own business when I was called back up because the billionaire wanted to talk to me. He told his wife to go inside and then said, 'Sit down, Niall.' That was about the first coherent sentence he had ever spoken to me, so I was taken aback.

As I sat down he pointed to the islands of the Bahamas and said, 'See all of this? It's all beautiful and I love every second of it but it isn't what matters in life, Niall.' He stopped and pointed at the boat and the luxury around us.

'This stuff isn't important,' he continued. 'I know I'm going to die pretty soon and I'd swap it all for just one week of being healthy back with my kids again. I know you'll be a success, Niall, and I just want you to remember that.'

I was absolutely flabbergasted and as his wife came back outside he said, 'I'm tired now. I need to sleep.' As I walked downstairs I knew I'd learned another fundamentally important lesson about getting the important shit done, but I have to admit there was also a part of me saying, 'Yeah, it's easy to give the lecture sitting on the back of a thirty-million-dollar yacht with twelve staff cooking you lobster every day.'

I don't know where those few sentences came from or how he got them out, but he taught me more in twenty seconds on that beautiful Caribbean evening than I learned in my twelve years in school. Life is about the journey we all take rather than some goal that we all chase. It's certainly not about money. Getting shit done for me has always been about living in the present and ticking off crazy dreams and goals every single day.

I'm not always the happiest person but I'm a firm believer that every single one of us can achieve anything we want. It starts right now. Not next month. Not for your New Year's resolutions. Lose the fear of failure. Enjoy every moment as if it were your last and, most of all, please start getting shit done.

He just wanted a decent book to read ...

Not too much to ask, is it? It was in 1935 when Allen Lane, Managing Director of Bodley Head Publishers, stood on a platform at Exeter railway station looking for something good to read on his journey back to London. His choice was limited to popular magazines and poor-quality paperbacks – the same choice faced every day by the vast majority of readers, few of whom could afford hardbacks. Lane's disappointment and subsequent anger at the range of books generally available led him to found a company – and change the world.

'We believed in the existence in this country of a vast reading public for intelligent books at a low price, and staked everything on it'
Sir Allen Lane, 1902–1970, founder of Penguin Books

The quality paperback had arrived – and not just in bookshops. Lane was adamant that his Penguins should appear in chain stores and tobacconists, and should cost no more than a packet of cigarettes.

Reading habits (and cigarette prices) have changed since 1935, but Penguin still believes in publishing the best books for everybody to enjoy. We still believe that good design costs no more than bad design, and we still believe that quality books published passionately and responsibly make the world a better place.

So wherever you see the little bird – whether it's on a piece of prize-winning literary fiction or a celebrity autobiography, political tour de force or historical masterpiece, a serial-killer thriller, reference book, world classic or a piece of pure escapism – you can bet that it represents the very best that the genre has to offer.

Whatever you like to read – trust Penguin.